FIRESIDE

Ardy Friedberg is also the author of
Weight Training for Runners
and coauthor of *The Mentzer Method of Fitness*

How to Run
YOUR FIRST MARATHON

Ardy Friedberg

A FIRESIDE BOOK
Published by Simon and Schuster
New York

Simon & Schuster Building
Rockefeller Center
1230 Avenue of the Americas
New York, New York 10020
FIRESIDE and colophon are registered trademarks of Simon & Schuster, Inc.
Designed by H. Roberts Design
Manufactured in the United States of America
Printed and bound by Halliday Lithograph
10 9 8

Library of Congress Cataloging in Publication Data

Friedberg, Ardy.
    How to run your first marathon.

    "A Fireside book."
    1. Marathon running—Training.   I. Title.
GV1065.17.T73F74   796.4'26   82-735
                                        AACR2
ISBN 0-671-44206-6

For My Mother

Contents

How to Run
YOUR
FIRST
MARATHON

Introduction

The fitness tide hit American shores in the mid-1970s and sent millions of people scurrying from the security of their beach blankets to the jogging trails, the gyms, the health clubs and the spas in a head-long dash toward physical well-being. Today, public opinion surveys estimate there are more than 90 million people exercising on a regular basis; and this group of fitness-minded people is said to include at least 20 million runners—men, women and children—who cover anywhere from 10 to 110 miles a week with a dedication and fervor that borders on the religious.

A substantial number of these runners compete in one or more of the thousands of sponsored races held each year from coast to coast. Most of these racers enter the fun runs of 1 or 2 miles or the 5- and 10-kilometer events (see Appendix for kilometer/mile conversion table); but the phenomenal growth in the number of these shorter road races has spurred a nearly parallel growth in long-distance racing—20-kilometer runs, 13.1-mile half-marathons, and the ultimate distance for most people: the 26.2-mile marathon. In 1981 there were at least 350 marathons staged in this country alone, and in 1982 there are nearly 400 officially sanctioned marathons scheduled. There is no way to accurately estimate the number of people expected to run in these races but it is safe to say that there will be close to half a million participants.

Statistics compiled by the running magazines and the Road Runners Club of America show that about half of the runners in every marathon are running the distance for the first time. This is remarkable considering the grueling image of the run and its reputation for reducing the legs of world-class runners to jelly after 20 exhausting miles.

Yet it's a strange fact of human nature that many brand new runners start to think about competing in the marathon before they've finished breaking in their first pair of expensive running shoes. There are undoubtedly an infinite number of personal reasons, conscious and subconscious, for this rush to tackle the fabled distance; but in the end most people do it for the pure challenge, the chance to do something relatively few people have done, and maybe to learn something about themselves in the process.

Unfortunately, most runners, new or old, really don't know much about distance running in general or running the marathon distance in particular, although they usually do have a crystal clear vision of cheering crowds lining the route, of gallantly sprinting the final 200 meters, and of crossing the finish line with their hands upraised in triumph. The novice will soon find, however, that the distance between that vision and reality is much greater than 26 miles, 385 yards. The road to that first finish line is not only several hundred miles long, but it's strewn with obstacles—rain, blisters, boredom, potholes, snapping dogs, fatigue, hostile pedestrians, depression, honking cars, sore knees, and a general weariness of mind and spirit that can force even the most determined runner off the path.

The truly committed runner moves through, over, and around these obstacles, tries to ignore the physical aches and pains, accepts the strain of hours of training time on personal relationships and job productivity, disdains thoughts of "The Wall," and begins to look at the training and the race as a personal assault on Mt. Everest, something that needs to be done because it's there.

The challenge is formidable, but it need not be a crusade, and it isn't necessary to destroy physical and mental health to achieve the desired goal. It should, in fact, be fun—a personal battle, to be sure, but with plenty of room for humor, insight, good sense and perspective.

How to Run Your First Marathon will help you meet that challenge. This book provides a realistic training program for people of all ages and athletic abilities who have decided to run a marathon. Everything is here and it's based on the most recent research in exercise physiology, sports medicine, diet, and nutrition.

1
The Starting Line

I was one of the 2 million or so spectators at the 1978 New York City Marathon. I'd been running for a couple of years but had never entered, or even seen a race. As I stood on First Avenue at 68th Street waiting for the leaders to pass, I couldn't help eavesdropping on the conversations around me. Most of the people seemed to know about the famous runners—Bill Rodgers, Grete Waitz, Kirk Pfeffer and the other favorites—and they talked knowledgeably about split times, training methods, and a lot of "runner-ese" that was meaningless to me then. I was impressed that so many people seemed to know so much about a sport that had remained in relative obscurity until Frank Shorter won the marathon for the United States in the 1972 Olympics.

As I watched and listened, the leaders came and went, running very fast. They were followed by a pack of good runners, also moving right along. Then the steady stream, more a river, of 7- and 8-minute milers began. I was thrilled by the spectacle of it all and amazed at the determination of the 12,000 otherwise ordinary men and women chugging past me, intent on running a distance few people would consider walking. I watched the never ending procession for more than 4 hours. As the 9- and 10-minute runners struggled by, I began to get a lump in my throat, knowing they were dog tired and still had nearly 10 miles to go. Then I got that anxious feeling in my stomach that always comes when I know I'm about to do something new. I walked home slowly, awed and inspired, and promised myself that I would run the New York City Marathon that very next year.

I trained on my own, putting in the distance and eventually working up to about 80 miles a week at an 8-minute pace. It wasn't a lot of fun; but I had been told, and I had read, that running the marathon was going to be an exhilarating experience filled with camaraderie, a sense of purpose, and topped by a feeling of personal accomplishment. I carefully prepared a race schedule that had my split times ("split time" is the time it takes you to run part of a given distance) down to the second for 5-mile intervals up to 15 miles and then I had the remaining distance broken down mile by mile. At the end of 5 miles the splits were worthless, but the overall training plan worked out fairly well and I finished in 3:41, about an 8:20 pace. But I wasn't happy at the finish. I hadn't counted on the last 6 miles seeming interminable, and I was physically exhausted. I told myself I'd never run another marathon. All the training, the boredom, the aches hadn't been worth it.

That winter I hardly ran at all. Then I began writing a weight-training book with Mike Mentzer, a former Mr. Universe. While researching, I discovered a good deal about weight lifting but a lot more about physical conditioning in general.

Winter turned to spring, and it came time to apply for the 1980 marathon. The memory of the previous year had faded sufficiently, and I began to train once again. But this time I was a lot wiser. I mixed my running with bike riding, weight lifting and brisk walking. I never ran more than 50 miles a week and cut my mileage back to 30 about 8 weeks before the race, although I continued to bike and lift weights. My training schedule was only a personal experiment, so I was prepared to drop out if it became clear that I couldn't make the distance.

The 1980 race was different. Unlike the year before when I lost everything at 18 miles, I was still going strong at 21 miles. Of course, as it must, the glycogen was finally depleted and the head had to take over for the muscles before mile 22. The point is, though, that I finished in 3:45 and in good shape. There was none of that nauseated, slightly faint feeling of the year before, and almost no soreness at all. I didn't even have to sit down, and mentally I felt as if I'd accomplished something.

Since then I've run dozens of races and I've done a lot more reading and research for the four books I've written on health and fitness. I now realize that I could have used a lot of help in preparing for my first marathon. I'll never be more than an average runner, an 8-minute miler at best, and as I look back on my training for the 1979 race, I can't help thinking how useless the books and articles written by "experts" can be for the person who has been running fairly regularly at average speed and has just made the decision to run a marathon. Almost without exception, these books are written for people who have their sights set on a 2:30 or 3:00 race, not for the 3:45 to 4:00 runners who constitute the vast majority of finishers in the open marathons. The only helpful reading that I remember was by Dr. George Sheehan—and his approach was more psychological and spiritual than physiological.

I needed real guidance and a realistic, sensible approach to training for, and running, 26 miles. And I know that there are tens of thousands of aspiring marathoners who need and want the same thing.

YOUR FIRST MARATHON makes the following assumptions:

1) You are already running from 5 to 20 miles a week, or you are in fairly good physical condition from other forms of exercise.

2) You have plans to run the marathon in the not-too-distant future and you could use some help getting ready.

3) You understand that this is not a fitness or diet program, although you will be fit and undoubtedly lose weight by the time you're ready to run the marathon.

4) You fully realize that there is no magic in any physical training program and that you have to stick with it over a period of time to develop and maintain your optimal level of performance.

5) You know that the approach used in this program has been developed through my own experience and is based on that experience and extensive research into exercise and fitness. Furthermore, you should understand that no exercise program is chiseled in stone. This program will probably have to be modified to meet your special needs.

With these points in mind, let's move ahead.

2
26 Miles Is a Long, Long Way

It's probably true that anyone in reasonably good physical condition can train for, and run, a marathon. But it's important for the fledgling long-distance runner to try and separate the glamour from the reality and take a long, hard look at a long, hard distance.

It's not easy to conceptualize 26 miles. It's an enormous distance to run—more than 46,000 strides. Maybe the best way to gain some understanding of it is to get in your car, check the odometer, and drive 26 miles around town. In the stop-and-go of city traffic it can take as long as 2 hours, but even at highway speeds, it can take nearly half an hour. Covering the 1980 New York City Marathon, a driver for a local newspaper followed the same route taken by the runners through New York's five boroughs. It took him 15 minutes longer by car than it had taken Alberto Salazar, that year's winner, to run the distance. When you've finished driving the distance yourself, look at a map and check the route you drove. Can you imagine walking that distance? How about running it? It's a task that keeps the average runner on the road for 3½ to 4 hours. National marathon statistics show that more than half the finishers in any marathon make it in just over 4 hours.

The body, the mind, and the spirit have to be highly conditioned to spend that much time running. And you'll find as you train that the body is much easier to condition than the mind and spirit. The body is definitely fatigued after running a long, slow distance; but it doesn't know if it still has 2, or 4, or 9 miles to go. Only the mind has that information, and it's tough to fool yourself.

So even though it's theoretically true that most people are physically capable of running a marathon, it's also obvious that marathoning isn't for everyone.

Here are some factors to consider.

WHO SHOULD RUN

Many former heart attack victims are confirmed marathon runners; even people with artifical legs have successfully completed marathons. Blind runners compete regularly, and there are many wheelchair competitors. But people with physical handicaps who do take on the marathon are highly committed and strongly motivated, and they are exceptions. Generally speaking, aspiring marathoners should be basically healthy with no major physical handicaps. Above all, you must have a sound heart and average lung capacity. Beyond these minimal qualifications very little is necessary, although it's probably wise to see a doctor before you begin this, or any, exercise program.

If you have a physical impairment or an illness, any and all exercise should be supervised by a doctor.* But before you give up the idea of exercising or running entirely, consider the fact that many doctors are now using exercise to combat chronic physical problems, from lower back pain to asthma, diabetes, and emphysema.

People who are heavy smokers or regular drinkers may find it difficult to train at first, but one of the beneficial side effects of running is the voluntary reduction in smoking and drinking that takes place when the runner realizes how these habits limit the body's physical adaptation.

Age is not a major consideration in long-distance running. All you have to do is take a look at the runners you see every day. People of all ages are out there putting in the miles. Runners in their 70s are plentiful and people in their 80s are not uncommon. In fact, the President's Council on Physical Fitness and Sports cites several studies that indicate running is "protection against the decline in work capacity normally evident with increasing age" and one 10-year study of 45- to 55-year-old men indicated running acted to "retard the aging process."

*Medicine and Science in Sports, 1978, contains the following statement: "Over-publicized marathon running by a few subjects [post-coronary patients] has aroused unrealistic expectations for the majority of coronary heart disease subjects and probably similarly for a considerable number of coronary prone subjects, many of whom have 'silent' coronary disease."

It's also clear that young children are capable of running the marathon. Although 5- and 6-year-olds seem to show no ill effects after long distance runs, the question of children running is still a controversial one—mainly because there is no conclusive research on the long-term effects, mental and physical, of long-distance running on children. The New York Road Runners Club has a 16-year age limit for runners in the New York City Marathon, and other sponsoring organizations have imposed similar restrictions. The questions about age don't concern the possibility of physical injury so much as the fact that younger runners aren't necessarily running for themselves but perhaps for their parents or coaches. Dr. Gabe Mirkin, a sports medicine specialist and runner says, "It is quite safe to say that children can run long distances without increased susceptibility to injuries." But he goes on to say, "If you ask me whether children should run long distances, my answer is that it's all right—if it's what the child wants. But I don't recommend it."

This doesn't in any way mean that children shouldn't run. On the contrary, their young bodies benefit from running in the same way that adult bodies do. But it should be left to the child to make his or her own decision about the longer distances, and the youngster would be better off competing against his peers than in adult races. Above all, kids should not be put in the position of having to please adults.

Women have as much stamina as men for running long distances. In fact, there is the strong possibility that women are more capable, physically and psychologically, than men when it comes to covering a very long distance with a minimum of effort and discomfort. Because a woman's metabolic rate is lower than a man's, she is able to run longer because she burns fuel more slowly. Even lean, healthy bodies have some stored fat; and women have more of it than men (approximately 25 percent of a woman's weight is fat—about 10 percent more than a man's). Fat is great long-term fuel. This is especially true in endurance exercise when the body starts to use fat as fuel. Many women finish the marathon distance with less fatigue. And women, although not as muscular as men, can develop strength (not defined muscles) very quickly with the proper training.

WHEN TO RUN

Beginning runners, and even more experienced runners, find it difficult to resist the magnetic pull of the marathon. The tendency is to start planning that first marathon as soon as it becomes obvious that you're capable of running 5 miles or more. The marathon dream doesn't present any problem unless there is insufficient time to train before the scheduled race, and this is true whether it's a first marathon or not. Some running books say you must have at least 1 year of running under your belt before setting out to run the marathon, and others say you need 2 years or more. This is a very conservative approach and perfectly acceptable if you can wait, but running is such an individualized sport that there can be no hard-and-fast rules.

It's entirely possible for an athlete in training to put in 10 to 12 weeks of serious running and then complete a decent marathon. Unfortunately, most of us aren't in training when we first start to run distance, so an accelerated schedule isn't advisable. If, however, you've been running anywhere from 10 to 20 miles a week for a few months, there is no reason why you can't start to think seriously about running that first marathon in 6 or 7 months and to lay plans for your training.

WHERE TO RUN

The Pikes Peak run is not a good choice for your first marathon. Neither is the Yonkers, New York, marathon. There are too many hills on these courses and too much danger of depleting your limited energy supplies. And most importantly, an exceptionally difficult first outing can end all incentive for a second try and sometimes the desire to run at all. If you've trained adequately you can probably finish a difficult course—but your body will suffer. So, it's prudent to select a marathon that covers a fairly flat course, one that's run in cool weather, and one that is close to home. You'll want to have friends and family out on the route to lend encouragement, to pass you sustenance as needed, and to meet you at the finish line.

There are more than 400 sanctioned marathons scheduled this year in this country alone, so it shouldn't be difficult to find one that meets these criteria. But if you should have to travel any distance to find the right run, be sure to plan on getting there at least 1 day early so that you can settle in and take a look at the course. It's good for you psychologically. And if you can, try to stay over the night after the race. It's good for you physically.

WHY RUN?

The "why" of running is an entirely personal matter. Putting in 20 to 30 miles a week is just fine for staying fit, and that's good enough for most people. But if you really want to run more miles for any reason, it's a good idea to plan on running a marathon because you'll need the incentive of an upcoming race to put in those hours and miles every week. Beyond that, every marathoner seems to have one or more good reasons for going the distance. The marathon is a happening, a special event, and that is enough to draw many participants. Other reasons range from the simple to the bizarre. Some runners wear strange costumes, some run for causes, some run because they've heard that a marathon is insurance against heart attack, and some run for the very personal and private accomplishment. But whatever the reason, it's important to go at it right and to come out in good shape. When you reach that point 20 or so miles out when you think you can't possibly make it, you ask yourself "why" again. You'll need that orienting vision to keep you going, and that vision will help you finish.

3
Taking Inventory

The death knell of most sports and exercise programs is unrealistic goal setting. You wouldn't think of picking up a golf club for the first time and playing 18 holes of par golf. The same is true of running. You shouldn't lace on a new pair of running shoes and expect to run long distances without adequate preparation.

The goal of your training program is to help you to finish that first marathon in good condition. It's an achievable goal if it's approached sensibly and realistically. You will run and finish the marathon if you have patience, perseverance, and the courage to resist the training advice of your friends, remembering that you are an individual and someone else's training routine won't necessarily work for you.

There are a number of elements involved in realistic goal setting—your current physical condition, the time you have available to train, your commitment to training, and the training itself. Let's look at them one at a time.

PHYSICAL CONDITION

There are only a couple of reasons why you wouldn't be able to run long distances: If you have a physical disability in the legs or hips, or if you have any kind of congenital heart problem, you are best advised to give a running program a hard second look and talk to a doctor. Otherwise there is really nothing to prevent you from getting started. You may be overweight and out of condition, think you're too old or too stiff, but these things won't prevent you from participating in active physical exercise. So many people have used sports activities, and running in particular, for rehabilitation that the idea that you are not fit enough to take part is much more an excuse than a reason.

It may help to take a little inventory by weighing yourself, taking your waist and hip measurements, walking up two flights of stairs to check your wind, and examining your diet. If you think you have any major physical problems, then see a doctor before you start serious workouts. Checking with your doctor is a good precaution in any case, and especially if you're over thirty. Most sports-medicine doctors recommend an exercise stress test for patients over thirty.

In any case, you are the best judge of your physical condition, so listen to what your body is telling you.

TRAINING EFFECT

You have probably heard about a physical reaction called the "training effect." It's directly related to physical condition and physical conditioning.

The training effect has come into prominence on the heels of the running boom, but its importance was recognized by Scandinavian physiologists back in the 1930s. You achieve a training effect for the heart and the muscles when you stress them past their current abilities. This means that if you run for 15 minutes a day, day in and day out, you won't stress your body enough to make the muscles stronger (including the heart muscle), and you won't increase your ability to run for longer periods. This is one of the reasons why people who work hard all day digging and lifting really don't show great muscular development; they are not increasing the stress from day to day. To achieve the training effect in running or in any other sport it is necessary to raise the heart rate to between 60 and 80 percent of its maximum ability to deliver oxygen to the bloodstream. When that rate is achieved it has to be maintained for anywhere from 12 to 20 minutes at least three times a week. The athlete who doesn't run, even someone as active as a squash player, never achieves a training effect because the duration of the *action* in most activities is too limited.

It's a good idea to establish your resting and exercising pulse rate at the beginning of your training. Either place your fingers on the artery on the thumb side of the wrist or on the neck artery in front of the thick muscle that runs vertically in the neck. After you find the beat, count it for 10 seconds and then multiply that number by 6. This gives you the rate for 1 minute. You can check your own heart rate by taking your pulse and using the following chart:

Heart Rate by Age

PERCENT OF MAXIMUM HEART RATE	20	30	40	50	60	70
60	125	115	110	100	95	90
70	140	135	130	125	120	115
80	155	150	145	140	135	130
90	180	175	170	165	160	155

The maximum heart rate is the number 220, minus your age in years, so that the maximum heart rate for a 30-year-old man or woman would be 220 minus 30, or 190. On the chart, 60 percent of that rate is 115, and 80 percent of maximum for a 30-year-old would be 150. This range represents the training zone, the level of intensity you must hold for 12 to 20 minutes, three times a week.

TIME

There is no point in fooling yourself. Training for the marathon takes a lot of time. Unless you work nights, you will have to squeeze your training into the early morning hours before work or after you get home in the evening. This isn't very difficult for daily training runs of 30 to 60 minutes, but in addition you'll have to save at least 1 day of the weekend for an extended run, especially near the end of the training period. As you'll see in Chapter Six's training schedule, you'll reach a point in the final 6 weeks when you'll need about an hour a day on the road and another half hour for cooldowns and showering. That's a total of about 10 hours a week.

PATIENCE

Training doesn't take a lot of skill but it does take a lot of patience. Physical development doesn't happen overnight (remember the training effect). It's a fact of life, nature, and physiology that it takes several weeks to build up to a point where you can comfortably run for half an hour or more. If you sprint out the first morning of your training schedule, you'll walk back a few minutes later wondering how anyone can hope to run continuously for 15 minutes. But, as you slowly progress, you will be able to feel the difference in the way you take on the day's run, and you will gain confidence in your ability to run for a long time. Give yourself time.

COMMITMENT

Everyone starts marathon training with a commitment to finish; but you won't know you're really committed until you get up one morning in the fifth week of training, look out the window to find a cloudy, misty day, and still manage to push yourself out of the house onto the road. At that point you will be over the hump, and the chances are good that you will make it to the starting line.

Eventually that mental act of forcing yourself will become a habit, but it shouldn't become a crusade. Marathon training should be part of your life, not your whole life. It's my opinion that if you let it become bigger than reality, you ought to drop the whole idea and take up racquetball or some other indoor sport.

4
The Need to Simplify

Here is an example of one of those impossible training routines I talked about earlier. It's designed for the third week before your try at a 4-hour marathon. It's taken from *Marathoning*, by internationally known track coach, Manfred Steffny.

Monday	2 x 6 miles in 57 minutes, 20-minute break
	(15-minute warm-up jog)
Tuesday	Rest
Wednesday	1½ hours of easy endurance running
Thursday	15 miles on the road in about 2:20
Friday	Rest
Saturday	1-hour easy run
Sunday	3-hour forest run with a 5-minute break every hour as desired

Henry David Thoreau said it best: "Our life is frittered away by detail . . . . Simplify, simplify." It would seem that distance running, one of the least complicated of all sports, would also be the easiest to describe and that training routines would be easy to follow. Not so. Most books about running, especially marathon running, are so esoteric, contain such a complex list of instructions, and create such a mystique about the sport that the average runner drops any plan before it is really given a chance. Some training routines are so complicated that you almost can't leave home without a mimeographed sheet of directions pinned to your shirt. The Manfred Steffnys, Arthur Lydiards and Ernst Van Aakens, though justifiably esteemed for their achievements in coaching competitive athletes, have raised training techniques to a high level of obscurity. They give you details that you don't need to know and inject ideas that needlessly complicate training. There are so many important things to think about at some point in your training that it doesn't make sense to waste any energy worrying about extraneous matters. Here are some things that are often stressed in running books—things that really don't count for much:

RUNNER'S TALK

A lot of people will tell you that you have to think and talk like a runner to be a good runner. My advice is just the opposite: Avoid runner's talk as much as possible. Virtually all the information you get from other people is worthless to you. What works for them, what is important to them, has no bearing on your training. I know that it's going to be hard to follow this guideline, but I can assure you that you'll be glad you did.

Prove it to yourself. Next time you're with a group of runners, listen carefully to what is being said without jumping into the conversation yourself. There will be talk about the best shoes, the best diet, the best warm-up exercises, the best liquid to drink, the best running clothes, and the best training methods. Everyone thinks he/she knows what is best. You'll quickly realize that most of what you hear is pure claptrap from people who have picked up their information from other runners or from books and magazines. It all may be very valid as far as they are concerned, and obviously they aren't out to deliberately do any harm, but unless you're careful, you may find yourself buying an unnecessarily expensive pair of running shoes, eating a diet of fresh avocadoes, drinking defizzed soda by the quart, and trying to run 120 miles a week. If you ask ten runners a question, you will get twenty answers on every subject.

Keep your own counsel, trust your own instincts.

THE MARATHON MYSTIQUE

"Running lifestyle," "holistic approach," "sacrifice," "pain," "dedication," "addiction" are all terms used to describe what it takes to run the marathon. There is a degree of truth in all of them, but this book is dedicated to the proposition that you can run your first marathon without forsaking your job, your family, your friends, or even your weekly golf game to complete it. You will have to make certain accommodations in your previous schedule, but marathon training doesn't mean a complete revamping of your lifestyle. Marathon training is only part of your life, not a lifestyle in itself, and it should be worked into your current mode of living.

Even nonrunners have heard about the "pain" of long distance running; and it has become one of the runner's commandments, "Thou shall endure pain." It's true that there is some pain involved in running, but there is pain in every other form of exercise if the activity is intense. The pain in running is no different, and certainly no more glamorous, than playing tennis with tennis elbow. It's all part of the mystique.

You will, of course, be fatigued after a hard workout, but fatigue is far from pain. Fatigue is the pleasurable, relaxing, and rewarding feeling of having used your body in a positive way. Pain has no reward.

SPLIT TIMES

Put simply, a "split time" is the time it takes you to run part of a given distance. Add your splits and you get a time for the entire distance. This allows you to know that you ran the first quarter mile in 2:00 minutes and the second quarter in 2:10 and so on. Are they important? Not very. Only the most competitive runners need to concern themselves with splits. If you're running 9:00- and 10:00-minute miles it makes no sense whatever to think of split times and even 7:30- and 8:00-minute milers are fooling themselves with splits. Trying to shave 10 seconds a mile off your best time may be a worthwhile personal achievement, but unless you have bigger things in mind the improvements in time are negligible for most distances and meaningless in a marathon.

LONG, SLOW DISTANCE

Distance does matter, but as you'll see later, there is really no reason to get caught up in the mileage, or the long, slow distance (LSD) game. Whether you run 1,000 or 500 miles in preparation for your first marathon is less important than putting in the time on the road. You will have to be prepared to run about 4 hours to finish the marathon, and that has less to do with mileage than you might think. If you get into the habit of running for a long time, you can also run a long distance.

DAILY TRAINING

Frequency of training in any sport is of critical concern. Professional athletes train in some way almost every day, and competitive runners run every day without fail. But you probably aren't quite that involved. Training needs to be a habit, but it's a habit that can be maintained with four or five fixes a week. If you absolutely have to run 7 days a week, those extra days of running should be shorter and less intense. There are other things in life besides running, and they should receive adequate attention.

TWO-A-DAYS

Some training books suggest dividing your daily run into two sections, running part in the morning and part in the evening. This is a fine plan for the competitive runner, but the first-time marathoner doesn't need that much work. Two-a-day workouts do two things for the average runner, both bad: they deplete your energy reserves; and they make you stale, dulling your desire for running in a short time.

INTERVAL TRAINING

If you like to run fast, you'll love interval training. Here's a typical day's interval training schedule:

Yds./Min.

2 x	880 at 2:45
2 x	440 at 1:16
4 x	220 at 0:35
1 x	110 at 0:14
1 x 1,320 at 4:30	
2 x 1,100 at 3:40	

Several fast 100- and 220-yard runs, separated by slow jogging or walking, might represent another day's interval training. Intervals are designed to improve speed, and they undoubtedly do; but again, remember that first marathoners are really not concerned with speed but with a steady pace and conservation of energy. Intervals are diverting and they do serve to stretch the legs, but they offer little racing return for the average runner.

"THE WALL"

"The Wall" is a theoretical point, out about 20 miles, where the body's glycogen supplies are exhausted and the energy to continue running is greatly diminished. It happens to everyone and it is a highly individualized problem, so there is really no point in wasting energy worrying about it. It's best to resign yourself to the fact that the last few miles are going to be tough but that you're going to make it anyway.

RUNNING STYLE

Everyone has a personal running style. A lot of energy can be wasted and injuries incurred by trying to change your natural form to match that of some other runner or the suggestions of coaches. You'll quickly find that you can't run very far on your toes, and that running while looking at your feet can be dangerous. You'll probably adopt a new way of holding your arms so that they remain relaxed, and you'll find that a straight back reduces fatigue and soreness. On the other hand, if you can run on your toes, look at your feet, be bent at the waist, and still run, that's fine too. If your style works, use it.

LACTIC ACID

Lactic acid is a chemical that builds up in your blood as you exercise. It eventually causes muscle fatigue, but there is no way to stop it so it's much like The Wall—expect it, but try to ignore it.

PERSONAL RECORDS

Personal records, or "PRs" as they're called, fall into the same category as split times. If you want to bother with them that's perfectly all right, but try not to be obsessed with the idea of PRs in training or in racing unless they serve as an incentive of some sort.

WARM-UPS

There are two schools of thought on warming up for long-distance running (see section below). One says that warming up is a must, and the other maintains that it doesn't matter. There is no scientific agreement on the necessity for warm-up exercises for running distance. And of course, there are warm-ups and there are warm-ups. I've seen warm-up routines that rival anything I've seen at the ballet. Carnival contortionists would be amazed that so many people can put their foreheads to their knees. In fact, warming up sometimes seems to be an end in itself, a creative, often bizarre, set of movements designed to loosen everything including the earlobes. Though such gyrations probably can't hurt, there is a growing feeling among coaches and exercise experts that they don't help much either. Physiologist Edward Fox says: "About half the experimental work has found warm-up to have neither beneficial nor detrimental effects. Because of the inconsistent results obtained from studies dealing with performance and warm-up, it is not possible to outline a definitive warm-up procedure."

In any case, the first 10 to 15 minutes of running at a slow pace will serve to stimulate the cardiovascular system and the muscles and will provide ample warm-up for most people.

For you, the psychological benefits of warm-up may be more important than the physical. If this is the case, then by all means, go right ahead and stretch, push-up, and sit-up. And if you can't live without the warm-up routine, keep it to less than 15 minutes because, according to exercise physiologists, any more than that is wasted effort and wasted effort is wasted energy.

CARBOHYDRATE LOADING

Carbohydrate loading—the practice of eating carbohydrate-rich foods like spaghetti prior to an endurance event—is still under investigation by nutritionists and physiologists. And although there seems to be some evidence that it works, there is no conclusive evidence on either side of the question. The idea is to pack energy-rich carbohydrates into the muscles to improve endurance. One of the world's foremost exercise physiologists, Dr. Per-Olof Astrand, says, "A varied, well-balanced diet in adequate amounts is all that is necessary from a nutritional point of view for the body to function optimally, and for providing a biological basis for top performance." Dr. Gabe Mirkin in *The Sports Medicine Book,* says, "Even with its side effects and shortcomings, a carefully controlled program of carbohydrate packing can help the performance of endurance athletes . . . ." There are obviously two sides to the story.

The real problem with carbo loading is not the loading side but the "depletion" side. Depletion is a very inexact process. A week prior to the marathon, the runner is supposed to work the muscles to exhaustion (deplete energy and glycogen) while limiting carbohydrate intake. This phase lasts 3 days and is supposed to keep the sugar content of the muscles low. The problem here is that you have to continue running although your energy level is very low and you never really know if you are depleting, or if you're just tired. Then the packing stage begins, and this is supposed to bind energy-producing carbohydrates (and therefore, glycogen) into the muscles. This is the fun part. But this phase has its problems also. It's very easy to overeat because your body is starved for carbohydrates and you can easily put on 2 or 3 unwanted pounds and get sluggish at the same time.

Carbo loading is another of those things you'll hear a great deal about, but your first marathon is not the occasion to try it. There are just too many other things to consider.

RUNNER'S HIGH

A lot of runners will tell you that they reach a point during a long run when they begin to feel euphoric and experience what has come to be called a "runner's high." There is some scientific evidence to support the existence of this feeling. Dr. Lee S. Berk, a preventive medicine specialist at Loma Linda University in California, has found that people who exercise regularly produce "high levels of a natural opiate called beta-endorphin." This is a hormone produced by the brain and the pituitary gland. It increases the tolerance of pain, it counters stress, and gives a general feeling of well-being. Dr. Berk concludes that this "may explain why people become addicted to exercise." It may, indeed, but runner's high isn't experienced by everyone and it isn't a primary reason for running. If you feel euphoric, that's great, but most runners think it's a highly overrated side effect of exercise.

RUNNING CLOTHES

You can spend a great deal of money on fancy running clothes and warm-up outfits, but it isn't necessary. Admittedly, the nylon running shorts currently available are comfortable, but those old gym shorts you've been wearing will do just fine. In cold weather a pair of ordinary cotton sweat pants will do the job perfectly. Clothes don't make the runner.

I realize that all these subjects have probably come up in your conversations with other runners and that some people undoubtedly put great store in their importance. But if we're going to simplify running and make it fun to train, these extraneous concerns can just sap your energy and divert your attention from the task at hand.

There are some things that do count very much, however. Here are some of them:

TIME

The training program advocated in this book is based on time—that is, the time you spend running, not the distance you cover. An hour on the road is an hour on the road, and it doesn't make any difference if you run 7½ or 5 miles in that hour. You'll be working toward the reality of 3 to 4 or more hours on the road for a completed marathon. That time is a guaranteed certainty (except in rare cases) and it should be your only concern. You are going to be building up a savings account of time, not of mileage. Start thinking now about doing your 20, 30, 45, or 90 minutes and forget about mileage.

WEIGHT

Your weight will have an effect on the amount of time you can spend training and on how you run the marathon. Weight is the mortal enemy of the long-distance runner.

Figure it out for yourself. If you are even 1 pound overweight, that means you are going to have to move that 16 extra ounces every time you take a stride—the equivalent of 1,700 pounds per mile. In training that's a lot of weight to move, and in running the marathon it can be deadly. There aren't many 6 feet 6 inch marathon runners because, even if they're slim, they still have a great deal of weight to carry. If you are overweight at all, you have to lose the excess—pounds equal minutes in the world of running.

A STOPWATCH

Because you're going to be running for time and not distance, a stopwatch is a good thing to have. Not that it's critical that you know the exact seconds you've run, but it will give you the minutes conveniently and make entries in your journal easier.

A RUNNING RECORD

You will want to keep a record of your running times so that you can figure out your weekly total. You may even want to put other things in your journal—weather conditions, route, mental attitude—but its primary function is for times. Don't bother with seconds; round your run off to the nearest minute. Here is a sample of the type of journal entry you might make:

Week	Date/AM/PM	Time	Weather	Route	Comments
4	7/20-A	20	Sun/85	Park	Easy Pace
4	7/21-P	15	Rain/78	River	Hard Work

GOOD SHOES

A good pair of running shoes is a necessity. Unlike special running clothes which you can nicely do without, good running shoes can make or break you. You can't run at all with sore feet or blisters, and shoes that fit poorly can cause both. Shoes with thin cushioning can cause knee, hip, and back problems. There are dozens of brands on the market, and most of them are good. Don't pay any attention to the shoe ratings because individual preference for feel and style are the only important considerations. Just make sure you get a pair with a cushioned sole and heel that will minimize the impact of each stride on your entire body.

RUNNING ROUTES

If you don't vary the routes that you run, you are liable to get as stale as you would by overtraining. Running laps at the neighborhood track may be convenient, but it isn't very stimulating; and the lack of scenery, and the monotony of circling and circling, can drive you away from training. Pick three or four favorite routes and then make variations in those as well. You're going to need all the visual stimulation you can get.

PACE

Pace is important because energy conservation is important. You have to condition your body to accept the stress of the pace that's right for you. This will take some experimentation on your part, but you'll know it when you find it—although your pace will probably be slower than you thought it would be. Most first marathoners aren't as fast as they think they should be, and there's absolutely nothing wrong with that. Acceptance of a slow, steady pace will virtually ensure a successful marathon.

STRIDE

You will develop the stride that's right for you eventually, although it may not be the same at 2 miles as it is at 12 miles. Your basic running stride shouldn't be too long or too short, because both efforts take extra energy and cause unnecessary pounding. It's best to experiment, and it won't hurt to vary your stride length during long runs to prevent tightening of the leg muscles.

LIQUIDS

The body runs on water almost as much as it does on food. It's absolutely vital to keep yourself well watered. The fact is, however, that unless the day is quite hot or very humid, you won't need to stop at every water fountain. On your long training runs of an hour or more you rarely stop for water, so it's obvious that you can go without drinking while running, at least for a time. On extended runs, however, it's a good idea to drink water before you leave and to replenish somewhere en route if you can. Unless the day is very hot, competitive runners, whose energy expenditure is much greater than that of the average marathoner, rarely take water during a race. They don't drink excessively, mostly because it slows them down. This is not a problem for most runners. Cold water can upset the stomach, however, and the sloshing in the stomach can be disconcerting.

OVERTRAINING

The biggest bugaboo in all sports is overtraining. When you put too much stress on the body, it breaks down. If weekly training gets into the 7- and 8-hour range, you are reaching the outer limits for the amateur—the point of diminishing returns, where every additional mile (8 or 9 minutes) of running will begin to tear down rather than build up.

It's common to think that if a little training is good, then more training is better.

But training too long doesn't permit the body to replenish its energy resources and can eventually prevent you from training entirely because continued excess stress will inevitably result in pulled muscles, strained tendons, torn ligaments, or worse. On those days when you feel really terrific and think you can run forever, resist the urge. Save it because you'll need it for another day.

WARM-UPS (AGAIN)

As I said, warming up is a subject that is currently in controversy. The positive side (see above for negatives) says that cold, stiff muscles are subject to strains, pulls, and tears when called on to contract quickly. Slowly stretching those muscles (for runners the hamstrings are particularly vulnerable), getting the blood flowing to the muscle tissue, pushing the blood through the veins and arteries to the heart, is beneficial. Physiologists recommend 5 to 7 minutes of stretching. The exercises should be slow and progressively more difficult—that is, requiring more stretching. If you warm up and then wait 15 minutes or more to start running, you'll have to warm up all over again because the muscles will have gotten cold.

COOL-DOWNS

Some kind of stretching exercise is necessary at the end of the day's training. It's probably more important than warming up. Dr. Fox says, "It is a common practice of athletes to perform light or mild exercise immediately following competition and training sessions. There is a sound physiological basis for such a practice: levels of lactic acid in the blood decrease more rapidly during exercise-recovery than during rest-recovery." Continuous movement in the same repetitious way also tends to tighten muscles. That's why you can touch your toes before you run but probably have trouble when you finish. Devise your own routine, but make sure you stretch the hamstrings and the lower back as much as possible. Ten minutes is adequate; much more than that is unproductive. (See Chapter Five.)

WEIGHT TRAINING

It's not true that running and nothing but running can make you a better runner. Running doesn't develop real muscular strength, and it doesn't do a thing for flexibility. Muscular strength and muscular endurance are the same thing. The President's Council on Physical Fitness and Sports says, "Strength development may be considered not only a physical fitness need but fundamental to the total physical being." Working with weights develops strength and—especially important for runners—develops upper body strength.

Working out with weights two or three times a week can be as important as your running. The right resistance exercises can build the upper body and provide the balanced muscle development that guards against leg, knee, and back injuries and prevents tightness in the upper back and shoulders that is so annoying in the latter stages of a long run. (See Chapter Eight.)

OTHER RECREATION

Running and more running can be deadly, and the same daily routine can eventually drive you away from training altogether. Do some bike riding, some swimming, play some tennis or racquetball. It's good for the body and the mind.

5
Warm-up Stretches

I'm sure you've noticed by now that when you first start to exercise you have a general feeling of sluggishness. That initial five minutes of running can feel like an hour, and it seems that your muscles will never get loose, your heart will never start pumping, your lungs never fill up. This is because the exchange of oxygen from the blood to the tissues and muscles is being adjusted to meet the new demands of movement. As your body temperature rises with movement, the exchange is more rapid and a steady state develops— oxygen intake equals oxygen outgo. This is what happens when you warm up.

As I said in Chapter Four, running slowly is as good a warm-up as you can get, but stretching exercises before running can also serve to get the blood flowing and the arms and legs limbered up.

Here are nine stretching exercises that will serve you well as a warm-up or cool-down routine. Do each movement five to ten times.

FOR THE LEGS

1) Stand about three feet from a wall with your feet about 12 inches apart. Put both hands against the wall at about shoulder height. Lean forward slowly until your elbows

touch the wall. Hold for a count of two and then push yourself back to the starting position.

2) Stand with your legs and back straight, feet close together. Slowly bend at the waist toward your toes keeping your knees locked. Grasp your ankles and pull your head toward your knees. Slowly uncurl back to the erect position.

FOR THE HAMSTRINGS

1) Sit on the floor with your legs straight out in front of you, your back straight, heels together and toes pointing down. Slowly slide the palms of your hands down your legs toward your feet. Go as far as you can, then grasp your ankles and pull your head toward your knees. Slowly go back to the starting position.

2) Lie with your back flat on the floor, legs stretched out full length, heels together, arms at your sides for balance. Slowly bring your legs up and over your head and try to touch your toes to the floor behind you. Hold for a count of five and return to the starting position.

FOR THE GROIN

1) Sit upright on the floor and put the soles of your feet together in front of you. Hold your feet together with both hands and try to press your knees to the floor. Then lean forward and try to touch your head to the floor.

2) Squat down with your hands on the floor between your legs. Move one leg back until it's fully extended. Your front foot should be flat on the floor and you should be balanced on the toes of your rear foot. Lower the back knee to the floor. Hold for a count of two and return to the starting position. Repeat with the other leg.

FOR THE KNEES

1) Stand upright, feet together, back straight, head up and arms at the sides. Slowly raise one knee as high as you can, grasp it with the hands and pull it toward the body. Hold for a count of one and return to the starting position. Repeat with the other leg.

2) Stand straight with your feet slightly spread and your hands on your hips. Bend your knees as if to sit but only go halfway down. At the same time, extend your arms in front of you for balance. Hold for a count of two and return to the starting position.

FOR THE ANKLES AND CALVES

Stand straight with your feet close together, your head up, and your arms at your sides. Raise up as high as you can on your toes, hold for a count of two, and return to the starting position. For added stretching action, stand with your toes on a piece of wood or a phone book. Raise as high as you can on your toes and then lower your heels to the floor.

There are infinite variations of these exercises and many additional stretching maneuvers that you can incorporate or substitute in your routine. The exercises in Chapter Eight can also be used. Just remember, don't warm up too long.

6
Training and Enjoying It

People are different and physiques vary greatly. There is the long, thin ectomorphic body, the more muscular and athletic mesomorphic type, and the bulkier, pudgy endomorphic physique. And, of course, there are infinite variations on these themes. Gross and relative strength also differ widely. And, as no two people are the same physiologically, no two are the same psychologically. Because of these and other factors—diet, nutrition, general health—no two people begin a running program at the same level of muscular or cardiovascular fitness. It's obvious, then, that no two people should train in exactly the same manner.

This chapter will give *one* training formula to help you prepare for and run your first marathon; but this particular program should only be used as a guideline. Some of it will probably fit your needs perfectly, and some of it won't work quite as well for you. If you find that it isn't working for you, then you can make the changes in the basic schedule that do work. The training schedule in this chapter is flexible and adaptable to any runner's level of experience, age, or sex. For example, if the first week's running times are too long for your current level of fitness, then cut them by ⅓. If they seem too short, try increasing them by ⅓.

Most marathon training programs are built on a 1- or 2-year training base, and almost all of them are directed at the experienced, competitive runner. This program is different. Because only 10 percent of all marathon finishers complete the distance in under 3 hours, it makes little sense to write a book for that one person in ten who doesn't need it anyway. Let Bill Rodgers and Alberto Salazar train their way and you train your way.

A 5-MONTH PROGRAM PLUS 2 WEEKS

This 5-month (20-week) training schedule is especially for the average runner. It's based on time, not on speed or miles covered. There is an assumption that you are currently running at least an hour a week; but even if you're running only 30 or 40 minutes a week, you can use the guidelines that follow. The training program builds to a 90-minute-per-week level fairly quickly and then adds minutes at a steady but easily achievable rate.

While you are building up your time, you will also be establishing a pace, or several different paces, that are right for you. In addition, you will be adjusting your stride and determining the best time of day for your running. Also in this chapter you'll find hints on how to run hills, mental games to play while training, suggestions on how to select the right training partner, and guidelines for recognizing the symptoms of overtraining.

75 HOURS IS ALL IT TAKES

In this 5-month program, there are 100 running days, and about 75 hours of running. For those people who like to deal in miles, this comes to about 535 miles at an 8-minute pace, 475 miles at 9 minutes, and a little more than 425 miles at 10 minutes. The training days generally alternate between hard and easy days, but 90 percent of all the running days will be no more than 70 minutes long.

I've selected time as the measuring stick for three reasons:

1) When running for time you don't have to consider distance. On days when you run 15 minutes, you simply go out 7½ minutes and back 7½ minutes. If you're running on a track you run as many laps as you can in 15 minutes and that's it for the day.

2) For most people, time is easier to handle psychologically. It's somehow easier to think of running for 20 or 30 minutes on a cold, dark morning than it is to think of running 3 or 4 miles. And you don't have to go through the inexact process of measuring every course you run.

3) Time is also different in another way. You don't have to give a thought to speed. Speed kills a lot of runners. Not literally, of course, but striving to improve your time can be discouraging and can ultimately cause the stress injuries so common to runners.

Schedule*
(In Minutes)

Week 1 Day/Min.	Week 2 Day/Min.	Week 3 Day/Min.	Week 4 Day/Min.
Mon. Off	Mon. Off	Mon. Off	Mon. Off
Tues. 10	Tues. 10	Tues. 15	Tues. 15
Wed. 15	Wed. 15	Wed. 15	Wed. 15
Thurs. Off	Thurs. Off	Thurs. Off	Thurs. Off
Fri. 10	Fri. 15	Fri. 15	Fri. 20
Sat. 15	Sat. 15	Sat. 20	Sat. 20
Sun. 20	Sun. 20	Sun. 20	Sun. 25
Total: 70	Total: 75	Total: 85	Total: 95

4-Week Total: 325

Weekly Average: 81

*This schedule is adapted and modified from my research, my running experience, and interviews with scores of runners.

THE OFF-DAYS

Like any exercise program, running can get very stale if you do it every day without letup. Knowing that you are going to have 2 days off each week, and knowing which days, can help you get out on those other days when you can think of a thousand excuses for not putting on your running gear. Monday and Thursday will always be off-days in this program, your rewards for getting out on the other 5 days.

Week 5 Day/Min.	Week 6 Day/Min.	Week 7 Day/Min.	Week 8 Day/Min.
Mon. Off	Mon. Off	Mon. Off	Mon. Off
Tues. 20	Tues. 20	Tues. 25	Tues. 30
Wed. 20	Wed. 20	Wed. 30	Wed. 40
Thurs. Off	Thurs. Off	Thurs. Off	Thurs. Off
Fri. 25	Fri. 30	Fri. 35	Fri. 40
Sat. 30	Sat. 40	Sat. 50	Sat. 50
Sun. 40	Sun. 50	Sun. 60	Sun. 60
Total: 135	Total: 160	Total: 200	Total: 220

4-Week Total: 715

Weekly Average: 178

ADAPTATION

By Week 8 you will be running more than 3½ hours a week, but if you've followed the schedule carefully you shouldn't have any problems. You'll find that once you've gotten ready to run, a workout of 30 to 40 minutes begins to seem like nothing at all. This is a good sign; it means that your body is adapting to time spent exercising, and that you are easily capable of doing more. You'll soon be at the point where overtraining can become a concern. When it becomes relatively easy to run for 30 or 40 minutes, it's natural to tell yourself that another 15 minutes or so won't hurt anything. And you're absolutely right: It probably won't hurt—and yet, it might. It's good to learn the discipline of training within your schedule and avoid deviation. Stick with the daily times, and if you want to put in a few extra minutes do it on your off-days—but do it sparingly.

2/6/94
12 WEEKS TILL MAY 1 — LINCOLN

Week 9 Day/Min.	Week 10 Day/Min.	Week 11 Day/Min.	Week 12 Day/Min.
Mon. Off	Mon. Off	Mon. Off	Mon. Off
Tues. 30	Tues. 35	Tues. 35	Tues. 40
Wed. 40	Wed. 40	Wed. 45	Wed. 50
Thurs. Off	Thurs. Off	Thurs. Off	Thurs. Off
Fri. 30	Fri. 40	Fri. 45	Fri. 50
Sat. 60	Sat. 60	Sat. 70	Sat. 75
Sun. 60	Sun. 60	Sun. 60	Sun. 60
Total: 220	Total: 235	Total: 255	Total: 275

4-Week Total: 985
Weekly Average: 246

PAGE 49 - 2 WEEKS TILL
PAGE 50 - 1 WEEK TILL

READ & FIGURE IF
IT WILL WORK
OUT!

LONGER DAYS

Saturday and Sunday [illegible] slightly longer and, therefore, harder days during the entire training period be[illegible] easier to find time to train on the weekends. Those longer times can be logged whenever you feel like it during the day. Then, of course, you have Monday off, so the [illegible] training effort is followed by a day of rest and [illegible]

Week 13 Day/Min.	Week 14 Day/Min.	Week 15 Day/Min.	Week 16 Day/Min.
Mon. Off	Mon. Off	Mon. Off	Mon. Off
Tues. 40	Tues. 45	Tues. 20	Tues. 25
Wed. 45	Wed. 50	Wed. 25	Wed. 30
Thurs. Off	Thurs. Off	Thurs. Off	Thurs. Off
Fri. 50	Fri. 60	Fri. 20	Fri. 25
Sat. 75	Sat. 70	Sat. 30	Sat. 40
Sun. 65	Sun. 60	Sun. 25	Sun. 45
Total: 275	Total: 285	Total: 120	Total: 165

4-Week Total: 845
Weekly Average: 211

CHANGE OF PACE

Weeks 15 and 16 are obviously much lighter weeks than the previous ten. You'd have to go back to Week 4 to find a lower total. This is done to prevent overtraining and overstraining the muscles and to provide a change of pace that you can look forward to during those hard days of Weeks 10 through 14. This kind of dip in training won't cause you to lose any of your foundation but it will ease the mind, allow muscles to recover, and give you some time to work other things into your day besides work and running. It will also make the next hard weeks of training seem that much easier.

Week 17 Day/Min.	Week 18 Day/Min.	Week 19 Day/Min.	Week 20 Day/Min.
Mon. Off	Mon. Off	Mon. Off	Mon. Off
Tues. 50	Tues. 50	Tues. 60	Tues. 40
Wed. 60	Wed. 60	Wed. 70	Wed. 45
Thurs. Off	Thurs. Off	Thurs. Off	Thurs. Off
Fri. 60	Fri. 60	Fri. 70	Fri. 50
Sat. 80	Sat. 90	Sat. 90	Sat. 45
Sun. 70	Sun. 75	Sun. 100	Sun. 150
Total: 320	Total: 335	Total: 390	Total: 330

4-Week Total: 1375
Weekly Average: 343

MISSED DAYS

During these 20 weeks there are going to be days when you can't run for some reason or other—business or family commitments, illness, injury. Don't worry about it. Even if you've only run 90 days out of the scheduled 100, you'll have developed all the stamina you need for the next step up in training intensity.

You can see that in Week 20 your running schedule drops markedly until Sunday. On that Sunday it's time for the 2½-hour (roughly 20-mile or 32-kilometer) test. Although it is not totally conclusive evidence, if you can run for 2½ hours, you are probably ready to run the marathon. It's also a good psychological test: not as difficult as running the marathon distance, but a real test of endurance nevertheless. If you aren't able to finish this long run the first time, follow the Week-20 schedule for one more week and try it again the next Sunday.

**Week 21
(2 Weeks to Marathon)**

Day/Min.

Mon. Off
Tues. 40
Wed. 45
Thurs. Off
Fri. 50
Sat. 45
Sun. 30–45

Total: Not more than 225

Repeat the schedule for Week 20 for every day but Sunday. If you want to try another 2½-hour run, go right ahead, but don't push yourself. You may want to prove to yourself that you can do it again (or for the first time), but your training has been adequate and there is no point in risking injury of any kind at this stage of training. Better to take a 30- or 45-minute jaunt just to keep loose.

Week 22
(1 Week to Marathon)

Day/Min.

Mon. Off
Tues. 15
Wed. 20
Thurs. 15–20
Fri. Off
Sat. Off

Total: Not more than 55

If your race is on Sunday, take Monday off as usual. On Tuesday, run easily for 15 minutes. On Wednesday, 20 minutes will be enough. You may want to run 15 or 20 minutes on Thursday. (If your race is Saturday, don't run on Thursday even though you may be anxious to get out there.) Don't run on Friday or Saturday. It will add absolutely nothing to your training, and now is the time to be seriously conserving your energy.

OTHER TRAINING TIPS
HILLS—THE UPS AND DOWNS

There is no doubt that running up hills is good training. It increases the intensity of your run and it prepares you mentally for the hills you will inevitably encounter during the marathon. For most people, running uphill is actually easier than running downhill. You naturally have a tendency to lean into the hill a little on your way up, and that's good; you tend to pump your arms more, and that also helps. If you shorten your stride a bit and slow your pace slightly, you should be able to maintain a constant speed (it doesn't have to be fast) and reach the top with plenty to spare. Remember, hills don't last forever, although they often seem as though they will; and when you get to the top, you can relax, breathe deeply and coast a bit.

Downhill running is a different matter. The problem is control. It's easy to get the feeling that nothing can stop you and that you can pull out all the stops. This isn't true. Pounding down a hill at full tilt puts tremendous pressure on your heels and uses much more energy than you might imagine. If you lean slightly forward and let gravity do its job, you will move faster and with less effort, but it's important to hold yourself back a bit and concentrate on maintaining an even, although slightly faster pace.

It's a good idea to practice running hills from time to time so that you can find your own groove. Experiment with several styles of chugging up and let yourself fly down to get that feeling. You'll probably find that you like going up more than coming down.

A TRAINING PARTNER

After you've established your own running style and pace and have been training for 20 hours or more, you may find it helpful to run with a partner. Running with someone, or a small group of people, does two things: It serves as an incentive to get you out for training, and talking to someone helps pass the time.

The problem is finding the right partner, someone who runs at the same pace and someone you can talk to easily for hours at a time. It shouldn't be a competitive situation where you try to race each other. You have your training pace, and you should not deviate; increasing that pace by even 20 seconds a mile can be taxing, and unfortunately the tendency is to run at the pace of the faster partner. It's also a good idea to run with a person who has more to talk about than running. You will exhaust that subject in the first couple of outings, and from that point on you should talk about other things and just let the minutes fly by. Finding this partner may not be easy; but if you do find someone compatible, you will reap the dividends. You might try the local Road Runners Club or the neighborhood "Y"s, even advertise in the paper if you're desperate. Just remember, for a few weeks, you'll probably be spending more time in conversation with your running partner than with anyone else in your life.

BOREDOM

Boredom is one of those things which running fanatics will never admit to; but whether they admit to it or not, long, slow distance running can be very boring. When you reach the dog days of training—6 to 8 weeks before the marathon—you will be spending more and more time on the road; and no matter how much you like it, no matter how interesting you find the scenery, no matter how determined you are to get those training minutes in, you are going to get bored and you'll need some diversion. Here are some suggestions for mental games that will help take your mind off the sometimes dreary sameness of daily running.

1) Try to remember all the state capitals of the United States.
2) Make as many words as you can out of the word *elephant*.
3) Say the letters of the alphabet backwards.
4) Make up limericks—"There was a young man from Kent," etc.
5) Go through the multiplication tables up to 15.
6) Name the first seven astronauts.
7) Smile at people and count how many smile back.
8) Count the number of lane stripes on the road.
9) Name the first sixteen presidents.
10) Hum or sing all the songs from *My Fair Lady*.

You should also be able to come up with plenty of ideas of your own.

OVERTRAINING (AGAIN)

Overtraining has been mentioned several times before, but its dangers can't be overemphasized. There is a natural and understandable tendency to assume that because a little training is good, a lot of training is just that much better. This way of thinking leads to running extra time and putting in extra days. Training too long and too often doesn't allow the body sufficient time to recuperate and replenish the energy resources expended. Training every day in any sport simply uses up the body's reserves. Physiologist Edward Fox says, "Replenishment of muscle glycogen in an athlete recovering from prolonged, continuous exercise is complete within 46 hours." That's a lot longer time than you'll be taking if you accelerate your program unwisely, and so your muscle glycogen will always be a little low.

Another effect, possibly more critical than the energy question, is staleness, or lack of incentive to run. This is very likely caused by chronic, low-level fatigue, and the only remedy is lighter training or a couple of days off. The symptoms of overtraining can include irritability, muscle and joint soreness, muscle pulls, and loss of appetite. But mostly, you just won't want to run. When running becomes a struggle, you are probably on the ragged edge and should cut back.

Work plus rest can often be the key to success. There are notable cases of well-known, competitive runners—Dave Wottle, Mike Boit, and many others—who have performed exceptionally well in races even though their training immediately before the event had been limited by injury or sickness. Overtraining is probably the most serious mistake you can make, even more serious than undertraining.

OTHER POTENTIAL PROBLEMS

Depending on where you run, you are bound to encounter some of the following hazards, and you should be ready for them:

Dogs: The best advice is to give *all* dogs a wide berth. Even the little ones can be devilish, and dog owners don't really seem to care much about runners. If you find yourself face to face with a vicious dog, you're going to be in trouble. Some runners carry sticks as protection.

Pedestrians: You have to watch out for people. They won't be watching out for you. It's much easier to run in less crowded areas; but if you must run on busy sidewalks or streets, then give pedestrians the right-of-way and try to anticipate any sudden moves next to you or dead ahead.

Vehicles: All motor vehicles are potential hazards. It's possible that some drivers intentionally try to harass runners; but more often than not, they simply don't see you, especially when rounding corners. Keep your eyes and ears open, always be on the defensive, and you shouldn't have any problems.

Bicycles: Bikers can be a major problem. Not only do bike riders have to be especially careful watching for cars and pedestrians, roller skaters, and skate boarders, they also have to watch for runners. There is little you can do except be on the alert and give room to maneuver.

Potholes: One misstep can cost you several hours of training time. It's not a good idea to look at your feet when you're running, but it is a good idea to scan the road several yards in front of you for major changes in the topography. Watch for puddles, as they can hide deep potholes.

Weather: During the course of your training you will have to run in various kinds of weather. In warm rain you will just get wet, and that's really no problem; but if the temperature is high or very low, dress accordingly. Always remember to dress more lightly than you would if you were just going out for a stroll, because regardless of how cold it is, you will work up a sweat and the more layers of clothing you wear the hotter you'll get. Maybe the most important item of clothing in very hot or very cold weather is a hat. It keeps the sun out in the summer and the heat in in the winter.

Following the schedule outlined above will help to get you to the finish line. The next step is a little racing practice.

7
Warm-up Races

Many people have been running for years and yet have never run a single race. Racing is simply not important to them, although running obviously is. Others don't run in any races except the marathon. In my opinion, it's important to enter a few easier races before running the marathon.

Racing can be an entirely different experience from training. To become a marathoner you must accustom yourself to the idea of competing and running in a crowd. Your first race will seem very strange, to say the least. It also may be the first time you have ever competed at anything, so it's better to start small. The milling crowd of runners, the jumbled-up start, the stop-and-go of the first few hundred yards, the jostling for position in the first mile, the pounding of thousands of feet, the labored breathing of the people around you, and finally the feeling of being alone in a crowd that comes after a couple of miles when you are working within yourself—all create an atmosphere that is unique to running.

Races also give you the chance to test yourself and your training, and to experiment. You'll learn what to eat before races (what agrees with your system and what doesn't), how and when to drink on the run, and how to handle the finish.

WHEN TO START RACING

Don't rush into running races. Make sure you have enough hours of training and feel psychologically ready to run and finish. Six weeks of running should give you enough time on the road to consider a short race. Don't try to run a race every weekend. There is a certain anxiety level that you don't need to experience, and besides, there is plenty of time to race.

WHAT DISTANCE TO RUN

In most cities there are regular races, and you should be able to find one in the 2- to 4-mile range. Don't try anything longer than 4 miles (32 to 40 minutes) the first time out. Gradually work up the distance until you can comfortably finish a 10-kilometer (6.2-mile) or 50- to 60-minute race. Stick to that distance for the rest of your training time. If you want to run longer times, then do it in practice. You'll get all the race experience you need at the 10-kilometer distance.

EATING AND RACING

In general, you should have something to eat before racing—but *the* something is important. Since the stomach and the intestinal tract are likely to react to your prerace level of anxiety, it's best to eat lightly and drink liquids that are easily digested. Most races are run before noon, so the meal you'll be eating will be some kind of breakfast. Eat at least 2 hours before race time. Toast with very little butter, fruit, some juice, a breakfast roll that's not too sweet will provide all the energy you need for a short run. Stay away from milk, grease (bacon, ham, sausage), eggs, French toast, pancakes, and other foods that are not easily or quickly digested. Try not to drink too much coffee because, although it may be a good stimulant, it also stimulates the kidneys. In brief, eat but eat lightly.

THE START AND PACING

You've been practicing your pacing, so you should know how you want to run; but running at that pace in a race will be difficult at first. The stimulation of the race situation, the sight of faster runners passing you, the general rush of adrenaline will induce you to take off at the start with the rest of the rabbits. This can be disastrous. You can easily leave your race at the starting line, be wiped out after 20 minutes, and end up dropping out with the uneasy feeling that this sort of thing is not for you.

As hard as it will be, start out slowly and work up to your pace more slowly than usual. Resist, resist, resist the urge to pass people running a little faster than you. It's sometimes painful to watch a runner old enough to be your mother or father leave you in the dust, but you aren't competing against anyone. You just want to run a race and see how it feels.

DRINKING

It's not easy to drink while on the run. Even experienced runners have trouble, and you will too. In very short races—2- and 3-mile events—there probably won't be any water stops even if the weather is very hot, but in the longer races there will be water every couple of miles. During your early races, take some water at these spots even though you may not need it. About half a cup is all you really need, so pour out the excess and it will be easier to handle. Slow down a bit so that your breathing will be easier, and then take small sips. Swallow and try again. If you are moving along, you'll undoubtedly splash water all over the place, but no matter. The idea is to get the feel of drinking on the move. Of course, you can always stop to drink. It takes a few seconds, but that won't matter as long as you don't try to make up the time too quickly. Remember: Sip, don't gulp.

THE FINISH

The finish presents some of the same problems as the start of a race. When you see the finish line there is a natural tendency to "turn it on" and sprint the final hundred yards or so. There is really no harm in stepping up your pace in the last quarter of a mile, but sprinting, though satisfying to the ego, has few rewards and may cause some problems. One problem is the possibility of pulling or straining a muscle during a finishing burst; but potentially more dangerous is the sudden stop that you must come to on the other side of the finish line. Just about the time your heart is really pumping and you're really flying, you'll cross the line, enter the finish line chutes, and stop dead. This sudden stop can cause dizziness and nausea because the blood is still flowing strongly and has no place to go. If this happens, jog in place, walk in circles, or do almost anything to keep moving. The feeling will pass as soon as your pulse rate drops.

Take some water after you've gone through the chutes and then keep moving for a bit longer. It's not a good idea to flop down. And don't hesitate to ask for medical assistance if you need it.

POST RACE

First and last: Take it easy. Pamper yourself a bit for the rest of the day. Even when you're used to running and in shape, racing puts a different stress on your body. Do some stretching before you go to bed to prevent any undue stiffening the next morning. You'll be surprised to find that although you haven't run any farther than you usually do, or possibly any harder, you will have expended more energy than you think. The recovery time will be short, but you will know that you've been in a race and that it was an experience different from your regular training run.

The warm-up races are not absolutely essential for marathon preparation, but they do give you the feeling of being in a race. If you live in an area where there are no regularly scheduled races, however, you'll still survive without any actual racing experience.

8
Training Without Running

It may be anathema to Dr. George Sheehan and other advocates of daily (sometimes twice daily) running, but there are alternatives to long, slow distance training and other ways to improve the oxygen-transporting system and to add muscular power and endurance at the same time. Weight training, biking, rope skipping, and swimming all put adequate stress on the cardiovascular system. Almost as important is the fact that they can be very refreshing variations of the sometimes deadly routine of run, run, run.

SPECIFICITY

Athletic training of any kind is specific. In other words, any exercise program designed to improve an athletic skill must include practice in that skill: You can only learn to hit a tennis ball by hitting a tennis ball. You may be able to hit it harder by strengthening your forearm and shoulder muscles, but strength won't help you hit the ball. This is true of running as well. Running up and down the basketball court won't make you a better distance runner. Even bike riding, which may seem to be quite similar to running, won't make you a better runner, although it will help increase your cardiovascular fitness.

The following activities will continue to build heart fitness and lung capacity while providing a good and useful alternative, or a supplement to your running.

Here are some brief workouts for each of these activities. Don't hesitate to substitute one or more on the days when you don't run, or just don't feel like running.

WEIGHT TRAINING

Probably the best type of exercise to combine with a running schedule is weight training. The right exercise routine can easily be substituted for a day's running, and a variation of those same exercises can be used as a warm-up or cool-down routine on any running day.

Professional coaches in all sports now say that strength may be the key to good performance because three of the elements common to good performance—speed, mobility, and endurance—are all functions of strength. For the runner, speed and endurance are of paramount importance. Weight training, the only real method of building muscular strength, can be the final element in a complete conditioning program.

Muscle fiber is torn during continuous, heavy exercise, be it running or weight lifting. Metabolic wastes of all kinds increase. Glycogen stores are depleted and blood sugar levels drop. Water is lost through sweat, and this loss can cause an imbalance in the electrolytes that are vital to the central nervous system. Joints, tendons, ligaments, and even bones are weakened. But immediately after the exercise is stopped, the body starts to reconstruct itself. It is this continuous process of tearing down and building up that creates the conditioned body. Working with weights has the advantage of increasing strength during the rebuilding process; thus it is possible to develop not only greater muscular strength and endurance but also stronger joints, tendons, and ligaments.

The following exercises will help increase the total body strength so necessary for stabilizing the pelvis, supporting the driving action of the legs and arms, reducing muscle fatigue that can result in stiffness in the shoulders, neck, and upper back, and supporting the tendons and ligaments around the knees and ankles—the high-pressure areas where sprains, pulls, and tears are common.

A basic set of barbells (about $25) is all you need for these exercises, and if you don't want to make that investment you can use heavy juice cans, an iron, or a frying pan for your weights.

These five exercises* take less than 10 minutes and can serve as either a warm-up before running or a cool-down afterward.

Remember: Start out with very light weights and gradually work up to heavier ones. Use a weight heavy enough to limit the number of times (repetitions) that you can do each exercise to 12.

SQUATS

Squats, or deep knee bends, may be the best single exercise you can do. They work the front and back of the thighs, the buttocks, and the lower back. They cause an immediate increase in the pulse rate because the body's largest muscles are being used. More importantly, squats strengthen the legs in a way that running can't.

Stand close to the barbell with your feet about shoulder width apart. Squat down and grasp the barbell with an overhand grip (palms down), hands shoulder width apart, and shoulders out over the barbell a little bit. Slowly raise the barbell in a line parallel with the body until you can tuck your elbows under it and raise it to chest level. Press it straight up from that point and then lower it easily behind your head until it rests comfortably on your shoulders and neck. Make sure that you're well balanced. Spread your feet and hands if necessary. Then, squat slowly as if sitting in a chair. Keep your back straight and your head up. Stop going down when your thighs are roughly parallel with the floor. Raise back up to the standing position. When you've finished your repetitions, take the barbell off your shoulders in the same way as you put it up there.

OVERHEAD PRESSES

The press, sometimes called the military press, is, like the squat, a good whole-body exercise, but it is especially good for the upper arms. Raise the barbell to chest level just as you did to get ready for the squats. When you feel steady and well balanced, press the barbell straight up over your head until your arms are fully extended. Lower it back to your chest and repeat. Make sure that your back is straight and your head up.

*Adapted from Ardy Friedberg, *Weight Training for Runners* (New York: Simon and Schuster, 1981).

FORWARD BENDS

This exercise puts pressure on the frontal thighs, the buttocks, the hamstrings, the stomach, and the lower back. Place the barbell on your shoulders as you did for the squat, and spread your feet a bit more than shoulder width apart. Keep the upper back straight and the head up while bending forward at the waist. Go down until your back is parallel with the floor, hold for a count of 2 and slowly raise back to the starting position.

POWER CLEANS

The power clean is the same as an overhead press, only the entire movement, from picking up the barbell to the arms-extended position over the head, is done without stopping. Pull the weight off the floor along a plane parallel with the body, tuck the elbows under and then smoothly press the barbell overhead. Lower it back to the floor for each repetition. You'll feel the effects of this exercise in the legs, arms, stomach, shoulders, buttocks, neck, and back.

DUMBBELL SWING

Take a dumbbell in each hand and raise to arm's length above your head. Spread your legs far enough to allow the dumbbell to swing through. Slowly swing the dumbbell from the overhead position in a wide arc, bend forward as the weight reaches chest level, and then continue to bend while swinging the weight as far between your legs as is comfortable. Follow the same arc and bring the weight back up to the overhead position. This movement exercises the whole body, but especially the back and the buttocks.

All of these exercises will add some needed muscle without reducing your running efficiency.

BIKING

To be beneficial, bike riding must be continuous—that is, you should have to pedal against some resistance most of the time without coasting. So try to find a bike path, park, or lightly traveled route with a combination of hilly and flat stretches.

If you have a ten-speed bike, shift into the highest (most difficult) gear and try to stay in that gear for most of your ride. Biking is only an adjunct to your running schedule, so don't try to put in 100 miles a week. When you do go out, however, strive for 30 to 40 minutes of good, hard riding (about 12 miles). You may want to start out in a lower gear to warm up, but shift into high as soon as you can. This kind of pedaling adds the intensity that is necessary to raise the pulse rate and achieve a training effect.

ROPE SKIPPING

Rope skipping is much more aerobic than it appears when you watch an expert doing it. Ten minutes of skipping will raise your pulse rate to near maximum and leave you feeling as though you've just sprinted half a mile. In fact, skipping rope is so good for the oxygen-transporting system that it can serve as a person's sole aerobic exercise with no supplemental activity. And it can be done anywhere. Skipping is also good for the arm, leg, and shoulder muscles and is a good warm-up or cool-down activity. You'll also be surprised when you discover that skipping isn't as easy as it looks. It will take some practice to get the hang of it.

Here are some helpful hints on jumping:

1) Jump in front of a mirror until you develop your technique.
2) Turn the rope with the wrists and forearms only.
3) Turn the rope as smoothly and steadily as you can.
4) Flex your knees.
5) Push off the floor with your toes.
6) Lift your legs high when jumping.
7) Land lightly on the balls of your feet.
8) Don't jump in bare feet.
9) Jump in an open, uncluttered area.
10) Wear comfortable clothing.

For all jumping steps, start with your feet together, back straight, with the arms extended and the rope behind your heels. Swing the rope up and over your head and as it comes in front of you, jump off the floor with both feet. After you have the rhythm, you can vary the routine by using alternate feet, running in place, and so on. Start jumping for 2 minutes and eventually work up to 15 minutes or more—the estimated equivalent of 45 minutes of running.

The quality of the rope isn't critical—almost anything will do. But the length is important; the ends should just reach your armpits when you stand on the middle of the rope.

SWIMMING

Swimming not only provides good aerobic work but also helps to build up those muscles in the upper body that are so often neglected by the marathon trainer. A half hour of laps will be a decent substitute for the day's run, and a lighter workout (15 minutes or so) is a fine addition to the day's run. Here's a 3-day-a-week workout that can be modified to meet your personal needs and capabilities:

1) Warm up for 5 minutes or about 200 yards swimming any stroke you like.
2) Swim 200 yards, resting briefly every 50 yards.
3) Swim continuously for 400 yards, rest for 1 minute, and swim another 400 yards.
4) Swim 100 yards three times using different strokes.

For variety use different strokes from workout to workout.

STAIR RUNNING AND BENCH STEPPING

Stair running is actually a combination of aerobic, anaerobic, and muscular exercise. Running up several flights is aerobic, one or two flights is anaerobic, but both are muscle developers. The steps in your office or apartment building are the perfect place to begin.

Stepping up and down on a sturdy chair, box, or bench is also good aerobic training. Five minutes of bench stepping will give you a solid workout.

RUNNING IN PLACE

If you can't go outdoors for some reason, running in place is an adequate substitute; but you must *double your normal pace* to get the same benefits. Boring, yes, but it's better than nothing.

STATIONARY BICYCLES AND TREADMILLS

Both of these systems will help supplement your training and are good diversions, but both are relatively expensive. If you use a stationary bike, there must be some method of adjusting resistance; and a nonmotorized treadmill should have an adjustable grade for it to be effective. Fifteen to 30 minutes on either device provide a decent workout.

All the activities outlined here are good for cardiovascular fitness and muscular development. They emphasize aerobic fitness as well and stimulate the oxygen-delivery system. They make the heart and lungs work harder to supply the working muscles with oxygen through the blood.

OTHER SPORTS

Other sports—basketball, football, the racquet sports—are good for general fitness, but they don't have the same effect on the oxygen-delivery system as those recommended above. Stop-and-go sports also pose increased danger of injury to the knees, joints, tendons, and ligaments. That is not to say that you shouldn't indulge in your favorite athletic activities—just be aware that these sports have limited benefits for runners.

9
Eating to Run and Running to Eat

There are some marvelous stories about the eating habits of runners, and a lot of them are true. There are runners who thrive on beer, citing the need for beer's carbohydrates while ignoring its calorie and alcohol content. Others seem to exist on a menu of junk foods that would be the envy of every dieter—pizza, donuts, potato chips, candy bars, and hero sandwiches. The remarkable thing is that serious runners can apparently eat and drink like Falstaff and not get fat, whereas most people have to struggle along to maintain or lose weight and are forced to eat a "proper" diet that can be not only unsatisfying but downright boring.

Without a doubt, good nutrition is essential to good athletic performance. The question is, then, do runners need special diets or dietary supplements to keep going as far and as fast as possible? The answer is an equivocal yes *and* no.

There are many nutritional factors that can affect your running, and they are worth considering one at a time.

CALORIES AND WEIGHT CONTROL

Many people have gotten caught up in the running and fitness craze because they want to lose a few pounds and have found that running is a great way to burn calories.

Calories are, quite simply, a measure of energy; and 3,500 calories are the equivalent of 1 pound of body fat. If you want to lose 1 pound, you have to cut your calorie intake by 3,500 or increase your energy expenditure by 3,500 while maintaining the same diet. If, for example, you cut back 500 calories a day (or increase your physical activity by 500 calories a day) you will lose 1 pound of fat every 7 days.

How many calories are you eating now? A good rule of thumb for most people is to multiply current weight by 15. If you now weigh 150 pounds, you are probably consuming around 2,200 calories a day.

Exercise burns calories, and running burns about 10 calories a minute. If you're running 30 minutes a day, you will burn about 300 calories in the process. When you increase your running time to 60 or 90 minutes, you obviously increase your calorie expenditure as well.

Those calories need to come from somewhere, but where?

THE BASIC FOUR FOOD SOURCES

The American Dietetic Association has divided commonly eaten foods into four groups according to their nutritional components. By selecting foods from each group, you will get all the nutrients to meet daily needs. Each group offers a variety of foods, so there is something for everyone's taste.

Vegetable and Fruit Group: Four servings a day will provide vitamins A and C, and fiber. Good sources of vitamin C are citrus fruits, melons, strawberries, cabbage, broccoli, peppers, and all dark green, leafy vegetables. Vitamin A comes from yellow fruits like cantaloupe, peaches, and oranges, and from dark green and yellow vegetables like squash, carrots, and broccoli. Fruits and vegetables also provide a variety of other nutrients including calcium and iron, nearly all are low in fat, and none has cholesterol.

Bread and Cereal Group: Iron, B vitamins, and fiber come from this group, and some protein as well. The foods in this category include whole grain and enriched breads, biscuits, muffins, cooked and ready-to-eat cereals, cornmeal, flour, grits, pasta, noodles, rice, oats, barley, bulgur, and tortillas. Starchy vegetables like potatoes, yams, corn, and peas also fall into this group. Four servings a day are sufficient. A slice of bread is a serving, and so is 1/2 to 3/4 cup of cereal, rice, or pasta, or 1 ounce of ready-to-eat cereal.

Milk and Cheese Group: Most of the calcium in the American diet comes from this group. Vitamin A is also provided by dairy products along with a variety of other nutrients, including vitamin D. An 8-ounce cup of milk in any form (whole, skimmed, buttermilk, powdered, or evaporated) or yogurt constitutes a serving, and you should have two servings a day. Two cups of cottage cheese, 1 and 1/2 ounces of hard cheese, or 4 and 1/3 cups of ice cream will provide the same amount of calcium but with varying amounts of calories.

Meat, Poultry, Fish, and Bean Group: This group provides protein, B vitamins, phosphorus and other nutrients; however, only foods of animal origin will naturally have vitamin B-12. Beef, veal, lamb, pork, poultry, fish, shellfish, organ meats, dry beans, peas, soybeans, lentils, eggs, seeds, and nuts fall into this category. Two servings a day are the recommended amount. A serving would be 2 to 3 ounces of lean, cooked meat, poultry, or fish, 1 egg, 2 tablespoons of peanut butter, or 1/2 to 3/4 cup of dried beans, peas, soybeans, or lentils. Again, calories vary.

Note: Some nutritionists put fats, sweets, and alcohol into a fifth food group. Such things as cooking fats, oils, butter, margarine, mayonnaise and other salad dressings, candy, sugar, other sweets and desserts, and liquor fall into this group. These foods are mostly calories with few nutrients. Vegetable oils do supply vitamin E and essential fatty acids, however.

You should keep the following in mind.

1) The Basic Four is a guideline for everyone regardless of activity level. (Obviously people have different activity levels and different metabolisms.)

2) The science of nutrition is very young, and until recently the focus has been on individual nutrients rather than on the foods themselves.

3) Foods contain many compounds which scientists are just beginning to understand, so don't think that a vitamin C pill every day eliminates the need to eat fresh fruit.

Let's assume that you have reached what you consider to be your basic running weight, that you are neither gaining nor losing, and that your energy level is relatively high. If this is the case, you'll be able to eat just about any combination and quantity of food you want, and vitamin and mineral supplements will rarely be necessary.

There are some factors that can affect your running, however, and some other physiological and nutritional facts that you ought to know about:

BASAL METABOLISM

The energy it takes to handle all the bodily functions, and to support life in general, is called the basal metabolism. The speed at which that energy is used is called the basal metabolic rate (BMR). The BMR represents only the body's basic energy needs, and it varies from person to person. When you move around, walk, exercise, or run, you create the need for more energy. When you're running long distances your needs can be quite high. If, as happens in some unusual cases, running cuts your appetite and you begin to lose weight, you may need to eat more nutritious foods; and in that case it's a good idea to look into vitamin and mineral supplements. Otherwise you may not have the necessary energy to continue training at an efficient level.

CARBOHYDRATES

Carbohydrates are primarily sugars and starches and are the body's main source of fuel. They have about 4 calories per gram and are generally found in the foods that taste good. They are considered fat producing. But, in reality, carbohydrates are vitally essential for energy, and about 50 percent of your daily calories should consist of carbohydrates.

FATS

The fats in the diet are a combination of chemical compounds that don't dissolve in water. They are very high in calories—at about 9 calories per gram they are twice as high as carbohydrates—and they provide some of the body's energy, especially after the carbohydrate supply has been depleted. Roughly 35 percent of daily calories should be fat.

PROTEIN

Protein (about 4 calories per gram) is an organic material used in the structure of the body's bones, cells, and tissues. The average person needs about 2 grams of protein per 2.2 pounds of weight each day, and that can be gotten from half a broiled chicken or 6 ounces of fish or a 6-ounce hamburger. Runners do not need more protein than anyone else.

WATER

The body is approximately 60 percent water. Water contains minerals and acts as a lubricator, a shock absorber between cells, an aid to digestion, and it's the body's principal means of cooling and maintaining normal body temperature. In the course of an average day, the body loses water steadily, and 50 percent of this loss is unseen. On a hot day it's not uncommon to lose 5 to 8 quarts of fluid, and this must be replaced by drinking and eating. A surprising amount of "solid" food contains a high percentage of water. Meats can be as much as half water, and most fruits and vegetables are 70 percent water. Ordinarily, thirst is a reliable indicator of the need for water; but this isn't necessarily true when running or exercising, so don't hesitate to drink even if you don't feel the need.

VITAMINS

Vitamins have no caloric value, but they do contain chemicals that are vital to your metabolism. Because most vitamins can't be stored by the body, they have to come from food, and the average diet does contain all the vitamins that you will need. Most nutritionists now say that extra vitamins or mega-vitamin regimens do not cure disease or improve health.

MINERALS

Minerals are passed on to humans through animals and plants. They are extremely important but are only needed in very small quantities that can be obtained from the daily diet. As with vitamins, eating extra quantities of minerals is unnecessary.

SUGAR

The U.S. Department of Health says, "There is a growing body of expert opinion that believes Americans would be healthier if they ate less sugar, not because it's bad for you, but because its only real contribution is taste and calories." Sugar equals calories. It has no other essential qualities, although in the form of glucose (in small amounts) it may help prevent low blood-sugar levels that come from prolonged exercise. Many nutritionists say it is preferable to get sugar from fruits, vegetables, and other foods of which it is a natural part. The Federation of American Societies for Experimental Biology has stated that the body has ample energy reserves and "because of these energy reserves, the argument that sugar is useful for quick energy needs before physical activity is discounted." This report would indicate that the candy bar pick-me-up is a wasted effort and adds little but empty calories to your body.

GLYCOGEN

"Glyco" means sugar. Carbohydrates are the body's main source of fuel and are stored in the muscles and liver in the form of energy-giving glycogen.

SALT

Salt has been identified by the U.S. Department of Health as a contributor to high blood pressure. Salt is a chemical compound of two substances—sodium and chlorine—that are dangerous to human beings in their elemental states. Sodium is a reactive, soft, white, silvery metal; and chlorine is a toxic, yellow-green gas. Of course, when combined, they are harmless in small quantities. Whether we know it or not, we eat about 2 and 1/2 teaspoons of salt a day, which comes to more than 8 pounds a year. A healthy person can handle this amount of salt, but there is evidence linking excessive sodium intake with hypertension (high blood pressure) which can lead to stroke, heart disease, and kidney failure. The Harvard Medical School Health Letter (1979) noted: "Few experts claim that salt (sodium chloride) is the sole cause of hypertension; rather, they describe salt as an important contributing factor in the 10 to 20 percent of Americans who are genetically susceptible to high blood pressure." Keep these facts in mind when reaching for the salt shaker, and remember that extra salt in the form of salt tablets *is not* necessary.

ALCOHOL

Alcohol, like sugar, is pure calories (about seven to the gram); but whereas sugar may have some energy value, alcohol has none. Even worse, it impairs your ability to process oxygen and it can cause coordination problems. Neither of these qualities is to be desired if you are planning to run or engage in any other form of exercise.

CAFFEINE

Caffeine, a stimulant and diuretic, is readily available in coffee and tea and some cola drinks. Dr. Edward Fox, in his book, *Sports Physiology,* says, "Recently it has been shown that caffeine can have a substantial positive effect on endurance performance." He goes on to say, "If a runner ordinarily takes 3 and 1/2 hours to run the marathon, ingestion of caffeine can cut his time by as much as 15 minutes. Caffeine seems to have a glycogen-sparing effect, in that it enables more fat to be used as a fuel, with less use of glycogen." Of course, caffeine also has a diuretic effect, so that too much coffee will probably force you to stop several times to relieve yourself and cost you that 15 minutes you might have gained. The best approach is to experiment and see if you notice any positive effects from the 100 to 150 milligrams of caffeine in a cup of coffee.

SPECIAL DIETS FOR RUNNERS

The reality is that there are no "special" diets for athletes. In fact, contrary to popular opinion, a person training for the marathon (or any athletic event) doesn't need anything special or more of anything, with the possible exception of calories.

Still, there are some things that need to be considered, and they could be thought of as "special" needs.

Energy: As you increase mileage, you may need additional calories. These calories should come from foods in the fruit and vegetable, and bread and cereal group, with an occasional extra serving of a dairy product. Don't fill up on fatty meats and sweets to make up the extra calories that you burn off.

Protein: Protein provides nitrogen and amino acids for the synthesis of various body tissues and for numerous other metabolic functions. During training there is a slight increase in the body's muscle mass, and the requirement for protein may also increase. Once that muscle mass has formed you won't need extra protein. One gram of protein for every kilogram (2.2 pounds) of weight is recommended daily. Studies on men performing heavy work have shown that 100 grams of protein (400 calories) is more than adequate. The American diet is high in protein, so supplements aren't usually necessary; also, excess protein can cause the kidneys to do more work, which in turn can lead to dehydration.

Iron: "Sports anemia" is a subject that is receiving more and more attention in medical literature. Exactly why this problem occurs in long distance runners is not fully understood, but iron loss can occur from excessive sweat, hemolysis (the breakdown of red blood cells), and gastrointestinal bleeding. Menstruating women have more of a problem. The symptoms of iron deficiency anemia are vague and somewhat unspecific but they include a general feeling of tiredness. A doctor can provide a simple blood test to determine the need for supplements. Red meats and organ meats (liver, kidney) are good sources of iron.

Carbohydrate Loading: Carbohydrate loading was mentioned in Chapter Four, but it also belongs in any discussion of food and nutrition, because no other aspect of the runner's diet has received so much attention in recent years. Some research has shown that increasing the muscle glycogen stores may improve endurance. "Loading" is a two-step process that begins about 1 week before the marathon:

Step 1) Three days of heavy exercise combined with a diet that is high in protein and fat and very low in carbohydrates. This literally starves the muscle cells and causes glycogen depletion.

Step 2) A 3-day diet rich in carbohydrates, which supposedly binds more glycogen than normal into the muscles.

Biochemically, the diet in the first phase mimics true starvation, and in a few days you feel and act like a starving person. In the loading phase, the proportion of carbohydrates is increased and fats and protein are decreased. Because the muscle cells are so starved for glycogen, they overcompensate and store extra glycogen.

You can test for glycogen depletion with keto sticks (available at any drug store) which test the urine and indicate the presence or absense of ketones. If ketones are present in the urine, your body is starved for carbohydrates and is burning fat so rapidly that incomplete products of fat metabolism (ketones) are "spilling" into the urine.

Per-Olof Astrand, the exercise physiologist, agrees that carbohydrate loading may be advantageous, but he adds: "It is more important, relatively speaking, to ingest carbohydrates during the actual event in order to supplement the hepatic sugar output." He suggests sugar solutions for this purpose.

You have to be careful if you take the carbohydrate path. It doesn't mean that you should eat more food than you normally would—but that you should change the ratio of carbohydrates in your daily diet. You may have a heavy feeling during the loading phase because water is stored along with the glycogen.

Remember, there is nothing known—no food, no pill—that will lead to exceptional performance.

10
Minor Injuries—
What to Do About Them

The runner's magazines generally devote half of each issue to telling people how to run and train, and the other half to explaining how to treat the injuries brought on by running—shinsplints, tendinitis, joint and cartilage damage, knee problems, bone bruises, blisters, and assorted other foot problems.

Unfortunately, statistics show that running is among the most dangerous sports, with nine out of ten runners suffering some kind of injury in any 12-month period. Some of these injuries are caused by stepping into potholes, collisions with cars and bicycles, and plain carelessness, but most are caused by running itself. It's really too bad that something so good for you can also be so bad for you.

Most running injuries are caused by force—the force imposed on the ankle, knee, hip, lower back, joints, tendons and ligaments as the foot strikes the ground. Each stride can create a force as great as four times your body weight; and obviously, the more you weigh, the heavier the pounding. In a way, it's no wonder there is so much talk about the "pain of running."

This doesn't mean, of course, that you're going to have any problems. You may be in excellent shape and just plain lucky. But in marathon training it seems that no matter how fit or how careful you are, you will eventually have to deal with a physical problem related to running—so you'd might as well expect them and know how to handle the minor aches and pains. Most injuries will be minor, and you'll be able to diagnose the problems yourself. If pain is severe, however, you should immediately stop training and see a doctor.

Some of the most common problems are:

MUSCLE SORENESS

It happens to everyone. Bill Rodgers and Grete Waitz run hundreds of miles a month and still have sore muscles from time to time. It's an amazing fact, but medical science has yet to discover the exact cause of muscle soreness. When you exercise vigorously, the muscles tend to stiffen and harden and become sore. The first symptoms usually appear about 12 hours after exercising. The pain often becomes more severe the next day and then begins to fade away.

Physiologists think that soreness is probably caused by tiny tears in the connective tissue of the muscles at the point where the muscles attach to the tendons. It's the repair of those damaged tissues that results in a stronger muscle, so the theory goes.

Rest is the only known treatment for muscle soreness—all the oils, liniments, and rubs notwithstanding.

BLISTERS

Runners usually get blisters (thin, rounded swellings of the skin containing a watery substance) on the toes, heels, and soles of the feet. Blisters are the result of friction against the skin and in most cases are caused by poorly fitting shoes. Large or small, they can be very painful and if not cushioned can force you to run unnaturally. This can cause problems that are much more severe than blisters. Blisters will usually break by themselves, and after they have drained, plain adhesive tape placed over the affected area will usually prevent new ones from forming. If you continue to have problems, stay out of your running shoes until the blisters have healed. If you have heavy thighs, you may develop soreness, if not blisters, on the insides of the thighs where they rub together. A little petroleum jelly smeared on the area before running will relieve problems in the summer, and panty hose will help prevent chafing in the cold weather.

CRAMPS AND STITCHES

A cramp is a sudden, involuntary muscle contraction that can cause severe pain. A stitch is also a sharp pain, usually in the side. Cramps and stitches can be mild or severe and can last for a few seconds, a few minutes, or even longer. Cramps can occur in any muscle and can force you to stop running entirely until the muscle loosens either on its own or by massage. But stitches, which usually occur just below the ribs, can often be overcome by slowing down and pressing your fingers into the body at the point of the stitch. If that doesn't help, stop, bend over at the waist, and breathe deeply.

SHINSPLINTS

Shinsplints vary from stress fractures of the tibia in the front of the lower leg to simple muscle pain in the same area caused by overuse. Treatment prescribed by sports medicine doctors usually consists of two or more weeks of rest.

RUNNER'S KNEE

This injury usually occurs in people who have been running for some time. The continuous movement of the knee causes a roughening of the underside of the kneecap. Again, rest is the only real treatment prescribed by doctors; but you can help prevent the problem by wearing good running shoes, running at least part of the time on softer surfaces, and avoiding running on angled surfaces like the shoulders of a road.

STRAINED MUSCLES, TENDONS, AND LIGAMENTS

These problems are usually more serious and can keep you off the road for a long time. Strains and pulls are usually minor tears of some part of the muscle fiber. Strains are more common in stop-and-start sports than in straight-ahead running, but long-distance runners suffer them as well. As in most cases, rest is recommended.

Note: It is a good idea to see a doctor if any of these problems is severe. Home treatment is fine, but avoid the temptation to get back on the track as soon as possible. Inadequate rest can result in aggravating the problem, possibly causing permanent, or at least long-term damage. Ignoring the pain of injuries and pushing through to the finish line is noble, but foolhardy.

11
Planning Your Race

Y ou have been training at a steady pace with little or no interval work and have been developing your own stride and running style, so you know how you feel after a half-hour run, after 45 minutes, an hour, and so on. In planning for the marathon distance and time, you will have to keep your pace in mind along with some other things as well.

PRACTICE ON THE COURSE

If you live in or near the place where the marathon will be run, it's a good idea to try out the course—not all at once, but section by section. You will not only get an idea of the time it takes to run certain portions of the distance, but also what the route is like—the surface or surfaces, the twists and turns, the hills (both ups and downs), and the scenery. Then you will be familiar with the course when race day comes around.

COURSE MARKERS

Most marathon courses will have markers at both mile and kilometer distances. The miles will probably all be marked; and there will be kilometer signs at the 5-, 10-, 15-, 20-, 25-, 30-, 35-, and 40-kilometer points. There may also be digital clocks at several spots along the course. You will have no trouble keeping track of where you are. In fact, sometimes these signs are uncomfortable reminders of the distance and time remaining. But they do allow you to keep track of your pace without constantly referring to your watch.

PACING CHART

The following chart can be used to check your progress as you practice on the marathon route and during the race itself. For easy reference, the times have been rounded off to the nearest minute.

			Miles			
Pace/ Mile	5	10	15	20	25	Finish
7.00	35.00	1.10	1.45	2.20	2.55	3.03
8.00	40.00	1.20	2.00	2.40	3.20	3.30
9.00	45.00	1.30	2.15	3.00	3.45	3.55
10.00	50.00	1.40	2.30	3.20	4.10	4.22
11.00	55.00	1.50	2.45	3.40	4.35	4.48

You can see that if you run at a 9-minute pace you will have covered 15 miles in 2 hours and 15 minutes and have only 1 hour and 40 minutes to go. If you're on a 10-minute pace, you will hit the 20-mile mark at 3 hours and 20 minutes and have only 1 hour left to run. As you know from your training, if you've run 3 hours and 20 minutes, you can definitely run another hour.

DIVIDE AND CONQUER

Psychologically it can be helpful to cut the race into smaller bits and somehow make the whole course look less imposing. The pacing chart can be used for that purpose. You can determine if you want to use all the course marks, just the odd numbers, or just the even, dividing and conquering each piece as you go. Of course, there are other, equally logical ways to divide the race. You may want to make it a series of 1-hour races, or 40-minute races, or you can divide it by neighborhoods, the spaces between spots where you know friends will be waiting to cheer you on, or whatever tricks you can muster.

THE START

The excitement of the start is difficult to anticipate. There will be hundreds of people, possibly thousands, gathered in a small spot, milling about, jabbering, bending, twisting, and generally champing at the bit. When the gun goes off, the leaders will sprint out and a number of people will try to take off after them. Don't get caught up in a racehorse start. You can easily throw the entire race away in a fast 2 or 3 miles that you haven't trained to run. Your energy won't be sapped immediately, but after an hour or so you will feel the effects of running too fast. If necessary, try to run at a pace slower than normal at the start, at least long enough for the fast crowd to spend itself. This won't hurt you in the long pull and it will do you good at later points in the race when you begin to pass people who whipped by you in the first few, hectic minutes. Be patient. Stick to your own pace.

DRINKING AND EATING

You should plan to drink one or two glasses of liquid, preferably water, before leaving home. This helps saturate the body and provides an instant reserve during the first half hour of heavy sweating. If it's a hot day you will need to drink often, but not necessarily early. Try to pass the first water stop unless you are really thirsty; and when you do make the first stop, look around to make sure that you aren't going to crash into someone in the crush to get close to the table. Move to the far end of the water area where there will be less congestion. Try to take only a few ounces each time you stop. If it's cool, you won't need as much liquid; but hot or cool, don't wait until you're dry in the mouth before drinking. The body begins to run dry well before the mouth does. Even if you're thirsty, however, try to avoid very cold or very hot drinks because they can upset the stomach.

In many races there are other drinks available besides water. One popular substitute, ERG, has additional electrolytes and supposedly provides more energy. ERG doesn't taste like water. It has a quite different, almost medicinal flavor, which can be a shock if you haven't tried it before. Use your practice races to test out the energy drinks so that there won't be any surprises on marathon day.

Official water areas are usually perfectly safe, but along the route there will be many well-meaning people providing a variety of liquid and solid refreshment. These unofficial concessionaires are generally as concerned with your health as you are; nevertheless, their offerings should be considered with care. There are a few nasty souls out there, and when you're on the run, it's hard to tell a few ounces of vodka from a few ounces of water. Unfortunately, a quick sip of alcohol can have devastating consequences. It's the same with food. Many people will have oranges, bananas, and other fruit to offer you, and some will have chocolate and hard candy. In the interests of safety, it's a good policy to accept food only from people you know.

THE LAST MILES

Some runners pass miles 17 through 21 without any major problems, and others will hit "The Wall" with a loud splat. There is absolutely no way of knowing in advance what your particular reaction will be. Interestingly, no matter what you hear about The Wall and what happens when you run out of glycogen, nothing can adequately prepare you for the experience. Your body may be wracked with excruciating pain, particularly in the thighs, your mind may wander, you may burst into tears, you may stop running and walk for a while simply unable to keep your legs moving. You may have violent mood changes that swing, almost minute by minute, from elation and a feeling of boundless energy to deep depression that sweeps over you like a dark cloud. The extreme physical and mental fatigue of those last 6 or 7 miles is something most of us have never experienced. Even the great runners have the same problems, and physiologists and nutritionists have not been able to come up with any solid answers to the problem. No amount of training, no special eating, no amount of rest or mental preparation seems to help in the final crunch. Additional water or a little glucose solution may be helpful for some people, but there is no proof that either will really replenish used energy stores. Possibly just knowing that you should expect a wholly new, and possibly unpleasant feeling is the best preparation.

The bright spot is that many people seem to recover, at least to a limited extent, after passing through the hard miles and actually pick up steam again with 2 or 3 miles to go. This lift is certainly something to look forward to. But again, everyone is different; so the reactions of other people may not be anything like your own. You may be one of the lucky ones who look back on the last few miles and wonder what all the uproar could possibly have been about.

COURTESY

The course will be crowded, at least until the pace begins to thin out the pack, so it's necessary to exercise courtesy and restraint. For your safety and everyone else's, look before moving from lane to lane, check around you before spitting, and if you decide to slow down, walk, or stop, slowly move toward the side of the road instead of suddenly stopping in the middle.

12
The Day Before the Day

The day before the marathon is a vacation day. Most marathons are run on Sunday, so you will generally have Saturday to get yourself mentally ready and physically relaxed for the big day. Take care of yourself, conserve energy at every opportunity, and use this 24-hour period for last-minute preparations.

Here is a list of "dos and don'ts" for race day minus one:

1) *Do sleep late.* At least stay in bed and stare at the ceiling. This may not be so easy. You're going to be keyed up, but if you think of the next morning and its demands, you may decide to remain stationary a little longer.

2) *Don't eat a big breakfast.* You'll be eating plenty later in the day. You don't want to load up too heavily on carbohydrates, because they will add unneeded bulk.

3) *Do drink plenty of liquid.* Try to drink more water than you normally do.

4) *Don't drink wine, whiskey, or beer.* Alcohol in any quantity will put extra sugar in your blood, add calories, and not do your head any good either.

5) *Do stretching exercises.* Stay limber during the day. A few stretches will make you feel as though you're exercising even if you aren't running.

6) *Don't run, not even 1 minute.* It isn't necessary, it won't help your body. Abstain.

7) *Do eat lunch.* At lunch you can start to load up a bit, but stay away from too much fat. You still have plenty of time to digest it before the race, but there's no need to make your digestive system work overtime.

8) *Don't talk to other runners about race plans.* Don't confuse yourself at this late date. They have their plans and you have yours.

9) *Do stay off your feet as much as possible.* Sit with your feet elevated if you can, but most of all just sit still. Don't do a lot of shopping or even casual walking around.

10) *Don't plan on going out that evening.* Stay home and have friends over, but don't go out. You could end up stuck in somebody's living room when you should be home in bed.

11) *Do try to keep your mind off the race.* Watch television, listen to the radio or stereo, read, play cards, and keep your thoughts far removed from the starting line.

12) *Do eat a good-sized dinner.* Don't stuff yourself but go back for seconds if you feel like it. The idea is to get full but not bloated.

13) *Do get your gear together and double-check it.* You will be much better off if you take the time to get things in order the night before. Don't leave anything to chance. You very easily could forget something important.

14) *Do go to bed early.* Stay up until 10:00, but that should be the latest. You don't have to go to sleep right away—and you probably won't be able to—but get in bed anyway.

15) *Do relax—you're ready.* It's hard to relax, and you may not believe you're ready— but you are.

16) *Set your alarm clock 15 minutes early.* This will prevent morning panic and give give you time to lie around in bed a little longer.

17) *Arrange for a contact person for race day.* Find someone you can notify by phone if you have to drop out of the race for any reason. People who are expecting to see you on the course during the race or at the finish line will then have a number to call if you don't show up when you should. This prevents needless and sometimes frantic worry by friends and relatives.

18) *Carry some money with you in case of a real emergency.* You may find yourself stranded somewhere out on the course and need to take a cab to get back to civilization. Be sure to have at least one dime for the phone.

You've now done all you can. If it's after 10:00 you should be in bed. Good night and good luck.

13
Race Day

Y ou will be up early the morning of the race regardless of the hour that you have set on the alarm clock. After all, you've been pointing toward this morning for 4 months, and the adrenaline is going to be flowing.

Follow the race-day plan that you've established in your warm-up races. Give yourself plenty of time to eat a light breakfast and go to the bathroom—and *do* go to the bathroom and go, go, go. It's a natural bodily reaction to stress and adrenaline flow—but by now you should know the story.

Check the radio for the latest weather report of the day and dress accordingly, remembering not to overdress. Carefully pin your number on the shirt that you will be wearing as you cross the finish line. If you take sweat clothes be sure to choose your oldest ones, because you may have to discard them either before or during the race. The same is true of gloves. Be ready to throw them away after you've gotten half an hour or so into the race. Take your time dressing, paying special attention to your socks (if you wear them), because you don't want any bunching up that can cause blisters. Make sure your shoelaces are in good enough condition to last the race, because there's nothing as disconcerting as a broken shoelace. Go through your bag once more and make sure that everything you need is there. If you're planning to check your bag in the starting area, be sure it is clearly marked with your name and your racing number.

If you're driving, get an early start. You could get caught in traffic somewhere or have car trouble or a flat tire, so leave extra time. If you are going with someone else, call him/her early and remind him/her of the scheduled departure time. If you're going by bus, train, or other mode of public transportation, give yourself even more time because you simply can't depend on things going right. It's much better to be overly cautious than to end up getting to the starting line 20 minutes after everyone else has gone.

BREAKFAST

Your stomach should be basically empty during the time of the race itself; however, a light meal 3 to 4 hours before the start can't hurt. Eat only foods that you have tried before your warm-up races—those that are easily tolerated and digested and familiar. Include some protein, a liberal amount of carbohydrate, and no fat if you can manage it. Large amounts of simple sugar aren't recommended either because they may cause a surge in the production of insulin and result in low blood sugar.

THE RACE

By now you have your race plan memorized so that you know approximately where you'll be at any given time. Nevertheless, check through it once more in your mind.

THE FINISH

You've planned the finish, just as you've planned and trained for the race, so you are in good shape when the magic line looms in front of you. Again, resist the urge to "kick it in." There is no need and your energy reserves probably are depleted anyway. And the crowd will be screaming and urging you on, so you won't have any trouble completing those last few hundred yards. Suddenly and finally, your dream will have come true.

You aren't quite through, however. After you've crossed the finish line there are some things to be aware of:

THE CHUTES

You will be finishing with a crowd, and even in the best-managed races the chutes can get jammed up. You may be belly-to-back in a line that seems to be standing still. Your legs have been moving for several hours, and they continue to need to move a little to keep the blood from pooling. Try to jog lightly, shake out your arms and legs, roll your head in small circles, and in general, keep the blood flowing. The line will eventually move and you will be out of the chutes and on your way to the recovery area.

CHAOS

The scene at and around the finish line will resemble a battlefield more than a sporting event. There will be runners gagging and vomiting, exhausted runners staggering into the arms of waiting volunteers, shivering runners huddled under blankets, runners hobbling on bleeding feet, the first aid tent will be filled with runners in various states of disrepair, relatives and friends will be frantically searching for runners, and everywhere there will be runners sprawled out on the grass, the casualties of the war of the roads. Be prepared for the sights, sounds, and smells of it all.

TAKE INVENTORY

The chances are good that you finished the race in fine shape, but it's a good idea to stop for a moment and take stock. After the first exhilaration of finishing, how do you really feel? Take a few deep breaths and check your pulse. Do you have any blisters, or slightly pulled muscles, or any problems you aren't familiar with? If all your parts seem to be in decent working order, move on to the reunion area and meet your friends.

MEDICAL ATTENTION

If all is not well, there should be a medical station, or some type of medical assistance at the finish line. If you have any problems—dizziness, fast heartbeat, bleeding blisters, stomach problems, overheating—have them attended to immediately. The medical people on the scene are highly qualified, often runners themselves, and they will understand your problems. There is absolutely no embarrassment involved. If you need help, ask for it.

DRINKING AND EATING

Even though you've had plenty to drink during the race, you will still be thirsty. Do drink, but stay away from very cold or very hot beverages because they can upset an empty stomach. There will undoubtedly be fruit and yogurt and assorted other light snacks in the area around the finish. If you're hungry, don't hesitate to eat, although it's probably not a good idea to gulp down five bananas in the effort to instantly replace lost potassium. Your body will be telling you something, so listen to it. Some people strongly recommend drinking beer at, or soon after, the finish. The theory is that beer has carbohydrates and therefore it not only satisfies your thirst but replaces lost carbohydrates at the same time. In all cases, eating and drinking should be done with some selectivity. Moderation is the key.

A FRIEND AT THE FINISH

Try to arrange for someone to meet you after you've filtered through the finish line process. You will want to share your experience, and you'll probably need a helper. Your friend should have a dry shirt and sweat clothes for you to put on immediately. Warn your friend in advance that you may not feel like talking or doing much else that's coherent for a few minutes but that you nevertheless appreciate the assistance. It may take you half an hour or more to get yourself moving, so he/she should be prepared to wait.

MOVING ON

Don't move until you're ready. You have set aside the rest of the day for recovery, reflection, and self-satisfaction, so there is no hurry to leave the area immediately. It won't do you a bit of good to bounce up and then fall on your face.

AT HOME

You will be stiff by the time you get home, but some of the stiffness and soreness can be eased with a good hot soak in the bathtub or a long hot shower. After hot water, a little light stretching may be in order, but only if you feel like it. Those first few attempts to touch your toes are going to be painful, especially in the back of the legs, so don't overdo it. A massage is a great idea if it's convenient, but just lying down and relaxing the mind and body for an hour or so will do you the most good.

THAT NIGHT

Plans for any post-marathon celebration should be flexible. It's entirely likely that you will want to eat and drink and have a good time, but it's also possible that you will be unusually tired and want to go to sleep early. If you feel good, then by all means, keep your plans. You have every reason to paint the town.

Note: Despite the best-laid plans, your finish might not be all guts and glory. You may encounter any or all of the problems mentioned above; although you shouldn't. If you're suffering at all, don't fail to seek immediate medical assistance. The first aid people are there to help, and they won't hesitate to summon special assistance for you if necessary.

14
The Next Day—
the Next Week

The day after your marathon is likely to seem like the proverbial "day after the night before." Your muscles are going to ache, your energy level is likely to be low, and you may be mildly depressed. Climbing or descending stairs will be difficult, and you may have blisters, shinsplints, black toes, a sore back, a stiff neck or a combination of all of them.

On the other hand, you may be just as chipper as you were before the race started. But regardless of whether you are up or down, sore or free of pain, the day after is still a time for recovery. Surprisingly, there has been little scientific research done on recovery time, but it is clear that several days of recovery may be needed to replenish stores of muscle glycogen and to remove the lactic acid from the muscles and the blood.

Here are some suggestions for the day after:

TAKE IT EASY

If your marathon was on a Saturday, you're lucky. You can use all day Sunday to pamper yourself in much the same way you did the day before the race. Sleep as much as you want, keep your feet on a footstool, get a massage if you can. If the day after is a work day, by all means go to work and bask in the glory that is rightfully yours. If your job calls for physical labor, then taking it easy will be difficult; but if you have a desk job sit with your legs relaxed and your feet raised slightly. Keep stair climbing to a minimum and stand as little as possible.

SORENESS

The muscle soreness you have won't go away for at least 24 hours and probably longer. Don't forget, you have just put in more hours of running than you have ever put in before. There is really nothing you can do to relieve the soreness. A little light massage of the affected areas won't hurt, but it probably won't help much either. Rest easy in the fact that the muscle pain will virtually disappear in less than 48 hours.

FOOD AND DRINK

At the rate of approximately 10 calories a minute, the marathon used up around 2,000 calories of energy. If the day was hot, you probably lost 5 or more pounds in addition to the calories expended. Most of the liquid will be replaced by your natural thirst, but don't hesitate to drink plenty of water and juice. You may not feel much like eating for some time after the race, but by evening you should be ravenous. As always, carbohydrates are the best source of energy.

EXERCISE

For some people, any exercise the day after will be too painful. Others may want to do some light stretching or some walking, and still others will get out and run a few miles. Your body will tell you what it's capable of doing; but I do not recommend trying to run any distance, playing tennis, or going bike riding. Any exercise that strains already tired and sore muscles will only serve to increase the intensity and duration of the soreness. You approached the marathon sanely, so don't be insane about running now. Too much too soon can put you out of action for several weeks.

And what about the week after? Two or 3 days off will put spring back in the legs and make running a pleasure again. And now that you've conquered the marathon time and distance, running 30 minutes will seem like a breeze. The question is, how much running to do?

You may want to start planning for another marathon, but don't think of running another long race for a few months. If you want to race, set your sights on a shorter distance a few weeks away. Then you will have an incentive to train. That race may be a revelation. You will probably find that your time for shorter distances has improved dramatically by virtue of your marathon efforts. It's not so much that you are a faster runner but that you know your limits, you know your body better, you know what exhaustion is like, and for shorter distances you know you can push yourself to run faster times without any physical problems. It's a great discovery, and it will reinforce your positive feelings about having trained for and run the marathon.

It is interesting that some people never run another race after their first marathon. They've done their competing, proved everything they needed to prove to themselves, their families and friends, and they rest on their laurels, moving on to other interests. But most people become inveterate runners after they have run a marathon and look forward to a long running future, with or without more races. This is one of the truly desirable side effects of marathon training.

The decision is yours, but whatever that decision, I hope you have derived something positive from your marathon experience. I know that you trained correctly, that you ran correctly, and that you finished in good shape.

And don't forget for a single minute that you've accomplished something that very few people can claim. You actually ran a marathon, all 26 miles, 385 yards of it.

APPENDIX A
Conversion Table

Kilometers to Miles
(1 Kilometer = .62 Miles)

Km.	Miles	Km.	Miles	Km.	Miles	Km.	Miles
1	.62	11	6.82	21	13.02	31	19.22
2	1.24	12	7.44	22	13.64	32	19.84
3	1.86	13	8.06	23	14.26	33	20.46
4	2.48	14	8.68	24	14.88	34	21.08
5	3.10	15	9.30	25	15.50	35	21.70
6	3.72	16	9.92	26	16.12	36	22.32
7	4.34	17	10.54	27	16.74	37	22.94
8	4.96	18	11.16	28	17.36	38	23.56
9	5.58	19	11.78	29	17.98	39	24.18
10	6.20	20	12.40	30	18.60	40	24.80

42.195 Kilometers = 26.2 Miles

APPENDIX B
41 of America's Most Popular Marathons

January

Mission Bay Marathon
P.O. Box 1124
San Diego, California 92112

Charlotte Observer Marathon
P.O. Box 30294
Charlotte, North Carolina 28230

Houston Marathon
12318 Nova Court
Houston, Texas 77077

February

Mardi Gras Marathon
P.O. Box 2232
New Orleans, Louisiana 70176

St. Louis Marathon
13454 Chesterfield Plaza
Chesterfield, Missouri 63017

Las Vegas Marathon
309 S. Third Street #316
Las Vegas, Nevada 89101

Trail's End Marathon
P.O. Box 7
Seaside, Oregon 97138

March

Booneville Marathon
118 E. Third St.
Booneville, Arkansas 72977

Maui Marathon
P.O. Box 888
Kihei, Maui, Hawaii 96753

April

Boulder Memorial Marathon
311 Mapleton Avenue
Boulder, Colorado 80302

Boston Marathon
Boston AA Marathon, Box 223
Boston, Massachusetts 02119

May

Avenue of the Giants Marathon
P.O. Box 214
Arcata, California 95521

Denver Marathon
P.O. Box 17382
Denver, Colorado 80217

Revco-Cleveland Marathon
P.O. Box 46627
Bedford, Ohio 44146

Track Capital Marathon
2055 Patterson
Eugene, Oregon 97405

Bolden Spike—Promontory, Utah
P.O. Box A
Brigham City, Utah 84302

Yonkers Marathon
Yonkers Jaycees, 10 Gladstone Place
Yonkers, New York 10703

June

Mayor's Midnight Sun Marathon
3960 Reka Drive
Anchorage, Alaska 99504

North Dakota Marathon
P.O. Box 1317
Grand Forks, North Dakota 58201

Race of Champions—Holyoke, Massachusetts
Two Progress Avenue
Nashua, New Hampshire 03104

July

San Francisco Marathon
P.O. Box 27385
San Francisco, California 94127

Big Island Marathon
P.O. Box 1381
Hilo, Hawaii 96720

Paul Bunyan Marathon
55 Washington Street
Bangor, Maine 04401

Grandfather Mountain Marathon
Box 90 B
Boone, North Carolina 28607

Cheyenne Frontier Days Marathon
1401 Dunn Avenue
Cheyenne, Wyoming 82001

August

CCAP Southern Illinois
Box 160
Flora, Illinois 62839

Oliver M. "Scotty" Hanton Marathon
2922 Pine Grove Avenue
Port Huron, Michigan 48060

Clarence DeMar Marathon—Keene, New Hampshire
P.O. Box 168
Gilsam, New Hampshire 03448

Hiberian Marathon—Ligonier, Pennsylvania
114 Greenside Avenue
Pittsburgh, Pennsylvania 15220

September

America's Marathon
676 N. LaSalle Street
Chicago, Illinois 60610

Heart of America Marathon
2980 Maple Bluff Drive
Columbia, Missouri 65201

Rochester Marathon
7909 Gembrook Drive
Rochester, New York 13207

October

Heart of San Diego Marathon
3640 Fifth Avenue
San Diego, California 92103

Golden Gate Marathon
166 Embarcadero
San Francisco, California 94105

Detroit Free Press Marathon
321 W. Lafayette Street
Detroit, Michigan 48231

New York City Marathon
New York Road Runners Club
Box 881 FDR Station
New York, New York 10022

November

Rose Bowl Marathon
235 E. Holly
Pasadena, California 91101

Philadelphia Marathon
515 W. Godfrey Avenue
Philadelphia, Pennsylvania 19126

Marine Corps Marathon
8th and First Streets SE
Washington, D.C. 20390

December

Fiesta Bowl Marathon—Scottsdale
4631 E. Thomas Road
Phoenix, Arizona 85018

Atlanta Marathon
3224 Peachtree Road NE
Atlanta, Georgia 30305

Honolulu Marathon
P.O. Box 27244 Chinatown Station
Honolulu, Hawaii 96827

The Major International Marathons

January

Hamilton, Bermuda
Hong Kong, China
Sea of Galilee, Israel
Christchurch, New Zealand

February

Beppu, Japan
Auckland, New Zealand

March

Shanghai, China
London, England
l'Essonne, France

April

Adelaide, Australia
Amsterdam, The Netherlands
Hamilton, Ontario
Debno, Poland

May

Vancouver, British Columbia
Jyvaskyla, Finland
Paris, France
Ottawa, Ontario
Galeta Island, Panama
Saskatoon, Saskatchewan
Madrid, Spain
Frankfurt, West Germany

June

Aarhus, Denmark
Sandbach, England
Winnipeg, Manitoba
Beitostolen, Norway
Otwock, Poland
Laredo, Spain
Dulmen, West Germany

July

Sudbury, Ontario

August

Shelburne, Nova Scotia
Stockholm, Sweden

September

Gjovik, Norway
Montreal, Quebec
Port Elisabeth, South Africa
Berlin, West Germany

October

Kosice, Czechoslovakia
Montataire, France
Athens, Greece
Dublin, Ireland

November

Rio de Janeiro, Brazil
Aarau, Switzerland

December

Fukuoka, Japan
San Juan, Puerto Rico

APPENDIX C

MARATHON TRAINING LOG
WEEK: _____

	Date AM/PM	Run Time	Weather	Route	Other Exer.	Wt.	Comment
Mon.							
Tues.							
Wed.							
Thurs.							
Fri.							
Sat.							
Sun.							

Total Time: _____   Weekly Average: _____

MARATHON TRAINING LOG
WEEK: _____

	Date AM/PM	Run Time	Weather	Route	Other Exer.	Wt.	Comment
Mon.							
Tues.							
Wed.							
Thurs.							
Fri.							
Sat.							
Sun.							

Total Time: _____   Weekly Average: _____

MARATHON TRAINING LOG
WEEK: _____

	Date AM/PM	Run Time	Weather	Route	Other Exer.	Wt.	Comment
Mon.							
Tues.							
Wed.							
Thurs.							
Fri.							
Sat.							
Sun.							

Total Time: _____   Weekly Average: _____

MARATHON TRAINING LOG
WEEK: _____

	Date AM/PM	Run Time	Weather	Route	Other Exer.	Wt.	Comment
Mon.							
Tues.							
Wed.							
Thurs.							
Fri.							
Sat.							
Sun.							

Total Time: _____   Weekly Average: _____

MARATHON TRAINING LOG
WEEK: _____

	Date AM/PM	Run Time	Weather	Route	Other Exer.	Wt.	Comment
Mon.							
Tues.							
Wed.							
Thurs.							
Fri.							
Sat.							
Sun.							

Total Time: _____   Weekly Average: _____

MARATHON TRAINING LOG
WEEK: _____

	Date AM/PM	Run Time	Weather	Route	Other Exer.	Wt.	Comment
Mon.							
Tues.							
Wed.							
Thurs.							
Fri.							
Sat.							
Sun.							

Total Time: _____   Weekly Average: _____

MARATHON TRAINING LOG
WEEK: _____

	Date AM/PM	Run Time	Weather	Route	Other Exer.	Wt.	Comment
Mon.							
Tues.							
Wed.							
Thurs.							
Fri.							
Sat.							
Sun.							

Total Time: _____   Weekly Average: _____

MARATHON TRAINING LOG
WEEK: _____

	Date AM/PM	Run Time	Weather	Route	Other Exer.	Wt.	Comment
Mon.							
Tues.							
Wed.							
Thurs.							
Fri.							
Sat.							
Sun.							

Total Time: _____   Weekly Average: _____

MARATHON TRAINING LOG
WEEK: _____

	Date AM/PM	Run Time	Weather	Route	Other Exer.	Wt.	Comment
Mon.							
Tues.							
Wed.							
Thurs.							
Fri.							
Sat.							
Sun.							

Total Time: _____   Weekly Average: _____

MARATHON TRAINING LOG
WEEK: _____

	Date AM/PM	Run Time	Weather	Route	Other Exer.	Wt.	Comment
Mon.							
Tues.							
Wed.							
Thurs.							
Fri.							
Sat.							
Sun.							

Total Time: _____   Weekly Average: _____

MARATHON TRAINING LOG
WEEK: _____

	Date AM/PM	Run Time	Weather	Route	Other Exer.	Wt.	Comment
Mon.							
Tues.							
Wed.							
Thurs.							
Fri.							
Sat.							
Sun.							

Total Time: _____   Weekly Average: _____

MARATHON TRAINING LOG
WEEK: _____

	Date AM/PM	Run Time	Weather	Route	Other Exer.	Wt.	Comment
Mon.							
Tues.							
Wed.							
Thurs.							
Fri.							
Sat.							
Sun.							

Total Time: _____   Weekly Average: _____

MARATHON TRAINING LOG
WEEK: _____

	Date AM/PM	Run Time	Weather	Route	Other Exer.	Wt.	Comment
Mon.							
Tues.							
Wed.							
Thurs.							
Fri.							
Sat.							
Sun.							

Total Time: _____   Weekly Average: _____

MARATHON TRAINING LOG
WEEK: _____

	Date AM/PM	Run Time	Weather	Route	Other Exer.	Wt.	Comment
Mon.							
Tues.							
Wed.							
Thurs.							
Fri.							
Sat.							
Sun.							

Total Time: _____   Weekly Average: _____

MARATHON TRAINING LOG
WEEK: _____

	Date AM/PM	Run Time	Weather	Route	Other Exer.	Wt.	Comment
Mon.							
Tues.							
Wed.							
Thurs.							
Fri.							
Sat.							
Sun.							

Total Time: _____   Weekly Average: _____

MARATHON TRAINING LOG
WEEK: _____

	Date AM/PM	Run Time	Weather	Route	Other Exer.	Wt.	Comment
Mon.							
Tues.							
Wed.							
Thurs.							
Fri.							
Sat.							
Sun.							

Total Time: _____   **Weekly Average:** _____

MARATHON TRAINING LOG
WEEK: _____

	Date AM/PM	Run Time	Weather	Route	Other Exer.	Wt.	Comment
Mon.							
Tues.							
Wed.							
Thurs.							
Fri.							
Sat.							
Sun.							

Total Time: _____   Weekly Average: _____

MARATHON TRAINING LOG
WEEK: _____

	Date AM/PM	Run Time	Weather	Route	Other Exer.	Wt.	Comment
Mon.							
Tues.							
Wed.							
Thurs.							
Fri.							
Sat.							
Sun.							

Total Time: _____   Weekly Average: _____

MARATHON TRAINING LOG
WEEK: _____

	Date AM/PM	Run Time	Weather	Route	Other Exer.	Wt.	Comment
Mon.							
Tues.							
Wed.							
Thurs.							
Fri.							
Sat.							
Sun.							

Total Time: _____   Weekly Average: _____

MARATHON TRAINING LOG
WEEK: _____

	Date AM/PM	Run Time	Weather	Route	Other Exer.	Wt.	Comment
Mon.							
Tues.							
Wed.							
Thurs.							
Fri.							
Sat.							
Sun.							

Total Time: _____   Weekly Average: _____